Hesiod and Homer wrote genealogies of the
gods for us Greeks, and they assigned the gods
their names, and explained their gifts and
skills, and described their appearances.

Herodotus, *Histories* 2.53.2

We poets made Jupiter transform himself into a
bird or shower of gold
Or plough ocean waves as a bull, with a virgin
on his back.

Ovid, *Amores* 3.12

Pro tip: if something in mythology looks simple
and clear-cut it's a TRAP IT'S ALWAYS A
TRAP THERE'S THOUSANDS OF YEARS OF
CONTEXT JUST WAITING TO STRIKE AND
CONFUSE EVERYTHING!

YouTube, Overly Sarcastic Productions,
'Miscellaneous Myths: Dionysus'

First published in Great Britain in 2024
by Ilex, an imprint of Octopus
Publishing Group Ltd
Carmelite House
50 Victoria Embankment
London EC4Y 0DZ
www.octopusbooks.co.uk
www.octopusbooksusa.com

An Hachette UK Company
www.hachette.co.uk

Text copyright
© Roman Mysteries Ltd 2024
Cover and interior artworks copyright
© Flora Kirk 2024
Design and layout copyright
© Octopus Publishing Group Ltd 2024

Distributed in the US by
Hachette Book Group
1290 Avenue of the Americas
4th and 5th Floors
New York, NY 10104

Distributed in Canada by
Canadian Manda Group
664 Annette St.
Toronto, Ontario
Canada M6S 2C8

ISBN 978-1-78157-949-7

A CIP catalogue record for this book is
available from the British Library.

Printed and bound in China

10 9 8 7 6 5 4 3 2 1

Publisher: Alison Starling
Consultant Editorial Director:
Ellie Corbett
Managing Editor: Rachel Silverlight
Editorial Assistant: Ellen Sleath
Copy Editor: Robert Tuesley Anderson
Art Director: Ben Gardiner
Production Controllers: Lucy Carter
and Nic Jones

All translations, unless otherwise
indicated, are the author's own.

CAROLINE LAWRENCE

PANTHEON

An Illustrated Handbook to the Greek Gods & Goddesses

Illustrations by Flora Kirk

To Melvyn Bragg and all the academics who have appeared on over a thousand episodes of *In Our Time*, a truly wonderful resource.

CONTENTS

FOREWORD

Recently, I listened to a podcast by two reviewers who went to see the Broadway musical *Hadestown* without knowing anything about it. They were surprised that most people in the audience seemed completely familiar with the world and the characters. The reviewers themselves knew nothing about the Greek gods and goddesses, or the underlying stories. They confused Hades, god of the Greek underworld, with the Christian Devil.

This guide is for those reviewers, and also for anybody else who wants a primer for the Olympian gods. I will attempt to take the richly complex characters of Greek mythology and boil them down to their broth-like essences. The stock cubes of gods.

But why? Why even bother to glance through a book on the gods? Because they still pervade our culture and it's good to know at least a little bit about them.

Put simply, the Greek gods were supernatural fictional characters that ancient peoples used to explain and control their world. The myths probably started out as etiological, which means they explained the origin of things. For example, why is the Earth bountiful for several months of the year and then suddenly stops producing? Why does water spring out of the ground in certain places? Why does that bird seem to be saying something to me? Why does that pattern of stars look like a hunter or a woman on a throne? How did the world even begin?

This may be how the first basic concepts of earth goddess and sky god came into being. The Earth produces things. It must be female. The sky rains on the Earth and helps things grow. It must be male. At some point, other levels were added: demigods, giants, nymphs, heroes and monsters. Almost every river, spring and ancient tree had its own associated figure, its own personified essence. Once you have named the god, demigod or spirit, you can approach it. You can worship it by bringing a gift or making a sacrifice. You can ask it not to hurt you. To benefit you. To protect you.

Persephone and Hades on a drinking cup *c.*430 BCE, British Museum

A WORLD FULL OF GODS

We move confidently through a mostly safe and hygienic world, thinking we are in control of our lives. The ancients believed in invisible spirits that could bring disaster upon them at any moment without the proper protection and propitiation. Their world was a complicated palimpsest with invisible creatures crowding thresholds, clinging to doorways, hiding under the sewers, lurking at the crossroads, looking down from ancient trees, looking up from wells, swarming through fields and floating in the streams. We wash our hands, look both ways and occasionally mutter a prayer. The ancients lived in houses full of decoration meant to keep away evil. They wore lucky clothing and jewellery, draped their children in amulets, made daily offerings to gods and demigods, celebrated rites and festivals of purification, rang bells, burned incense and used protective gestures and exclamations. They adorned their household utensils with anti-demon devices and uttered a prayer every time they stepped across a boundary or threshold, right foot first. There might be an ithyphallic herm (a simple anthropomorphic pillar with an erect phallus) to protect the outside of their house. Or a mosaic with an apotropaic image intended to prevent evil in the same place we would put a welcome mat. To quote a Jewish traveller, St Paul the Apostle, writing in the 1st century CE, '[w]hat is seen is temporary, but what is unseen is eternal' (2 Corinthians 4.18).

As human society evolved, the gods and goddesses reflected human behaviour. People moulded gods in their image. The masculine sky god became the patriarch, the head of the family. The earth goddess became the queen of the gods, the matriarch, in charge of marital harmony, childbirth and plenty. The clever unmarried aunt is the virgin goddess of weaving and warfare. The hot-tempered uncle who likes to fight is the warrior god. So we created craftsmen gods, merchant gods, shepherd gods. Divinities presiding over music, drama, sickness, health, agriculture, birth and death.

Where did they live, those deities not attached to a particular tree, spring or glade? Ancient Greeks believed they lived on the highest mountain in northern Greece: Olympus. And so they are called the Olympian gods. Even before Greece ceded world power to Rome, the Romans had adopted these gods or melded them with their own, usually renaming them in the process. Today we call them Graeco-Roman.

Cities and city-states adopted their own god or goddess. Cults grew in popularity, waxing and waning over time and space. Eventually, humans no longer needed or wanted the Graeco-Roman deities the way they used to.

Divested of their original function, the Graeco-Roman gods took on new roles, as archetypes. Today they are the cast of a new fictional universe that you could call the Olympians. They have taken their places alongside Harry Potter, James Bond, Indiana Jones and the characters of the Marvel and DC universes, *Star Wars*, *The Lord of the Rings*, and so many more. We keep recasting them, reimagining them, rebooting them. Because the gods and goddesses are archetypal, they can wear any clothes and exist in any society. We can relate to them. To paraphrase the French philosopher Claude Lévi-Strauss, the Greek gods are 'good to think with'. A recent spate of novels, graphic novels and musicals about them explore topics like sexual abuse, body dysmorphia and gender confusion.

So here is a compendium of Greek goddesses and gods explaining their origins, their attributes, their special talents, and also the role they play in modern storytelling and fiction. The illustrations are based on a selection of images from antiquity: depictions found on altars, vases, walls, paintings, jewellery and household objects.

WHAT EVEN IS A PANTHEON?

Pantheon is a Greek word for 'all gods' (*pan* = all; *theon* = of the gods). The Greek pantheon consisted of hundreds of gods but 12 were thought to rule them, the so-called Olympians. In fact, there were more than 12. The Greeks liked the number 12, so they added or switched gods, according to their preference. For example, Hades was one of the six children of Rhea and Cronus but because he dwells in the underworld he does not usually feature on the list. Poseidon, on the other hand, spends most of his time in the sea and yet he is considered an Olympian. Hestia, a modest goddess with no exciting stories, often gives place to Dionysus, the charismatic god of wine.

This book will cover all 14 Olympians and try to mention the most prominent of the other gods, as well as some heroes, heroines and monsters. I ask forgiveness from the gods and goddesses, heroes and heroines I haven't been able to mention.

THE OLYMPIANS

ZEUS

(ROMAN JUPITER OR JOVE)
'King of the Gods'
The archetypal PATRIARCH

ORIGIN STORY: Zeus is the youngest son of Cronus and Rhea – both Titans (see page 103). Cronus kept swallowing the children Rhea bore him so they wouldn't grow up and depose him, as he had deposed his father. By the time Zeus, the sixth child, came along, Rhea took action. She presented Cronus with a rock wrapped in swaddling clothes to make it look like a baby. Cronus swallowed it in one gulp. Baby Zeus was raised in secret. Later, after he had grown up, he freed his brothers and sisters from Cronus' stomach with his mother's help. Then he deposed his father and used lots drawn from a helmet to divide the world between himself and his two brothers. Zeus got the nicest bit, the sky, and demonstrated his sky-god powers by means of thunder, lightning, hail and rain.

JOB DESCRIPTION: sky god, king of the gods, judge, patriarch par excellence, unfaithful husband, serial seducer, master of disguise and showrunner of the affairs of men.

GOD OF: thunder, lightning, hail, rain, judgement, kings, rulers, emperors, lawmakers, judges, bureaucrats, those who want justice, including animals, and especially suppliants.

SIGNIFICANT OTHERS: His wife was Hera, but Zeus had many lovers: Alcmene, Danaë, Demeter, Europa, Io, Leda, Leto, Metis, Mnemosyne, Semele, Themis, countless nymphs and even some adolescent boys, including the Trojan prince Ganymede.

~

Zeus was snowing.
Aesop's Fables,
'The Goatherd and the Wild Goats'

~

APPEARANCE: He is often shown seated on a throne. He has a stern brow, long dark hair, a full dark beard, voluminous robes and a staff of authority or thunderbolt. He sometimes wears a crown or garland of oak leaves. In a painting by the 19th-century French artist Jean-Auguste-Dominique Ingres, he resembles Jim Morrison, lead singer of The Doors.

EPITHETS: Father of Gods and Men, Dark-clouded Son of Cronus, Aegis-Bearer, Delighting in Thunder, All-Wise, Averter of Flies and so on.

ANIMAL & PLANT ASSOCIATIONS: eagle, bull, swan, oak, olive.

WHERE TO FIND HIM: One of his most important places was Olympia, in the Peloponnese, where the famous Olympic Games were held every four years. The massive gold-and-ivory statue of him was considered one of the Seven Wonders of the World. Sadly, nothing of it remains today. Another site he is associated with is Dodona, in Epirus, where he spoke to priests and priestesses via the rustling of sacred oak trees.

In his Roman guise as Jupiter, he had temples all over the Roman Empire because he was the chief god who kept everything running smoothly. Roman Jupiter often shared temples with his wife Juno and daughter Minerva. They were known as the Capitoline Triad, after their main residence on the Capitoline Hill.

EPITHETS

An epithet is an adjective or descriptive phrase. Homer and other poets apply epithets to gods, heroes and even objects. These epithets help the poet keep to the metre, but they also reveal the essence of the person or thing. For example, Achilles is 'swift-footed' even when sulking in his quarters. Dawn is almost always *rhododactylos*, 'rosy-fingered', and the sea is *oinops*, 'wine-dark'. It can also be 'barren' because, even though it teems with life, you cannot grow anything on its surface.

The origins of some epithets could be mysterious, even to the ancients. Nobody could agree on why Athena is *tritogenia*. Does it mean 'born three times' or 'raised on the banks of a river called Triton'? Nobody knew for sure. It may be that you could make up an epithet. Plagued by flies as he made a sacrifice, Heracles called upon Zeus, Averter of Flies (Pausanias 5.14.1). This also suggests that you chose the epithet of a god or goddess to show which of their aspects you most required.

ONE OF HIS BEST-KNOWN MYTHS: 'Leda and the Swan'. Although married to his sister Hera, Zeus had many affairs, many of them non-consensual, showing that #MeToo is nothing new. His seductions were disturbingly creative. Zeus took the form of men, women, animals, birds, and once even a shower of gold. Zeus wasn't choosy. He was attracted to goddesses, nymphs, girls and boys. Leda was one of his many sexual conquests. Zeus took the form of a swan to seduce her. This memorable scene appears on ancient Greek vases, Roman frescoes, jewellery, mosaics and oil lamps. Hundreds of artists have painted or sculpted it, including Leonardo, Michelangelo, François Boucher and Paul Cézanne. Some depict Leda as willing, others not.

The offspring of this union is Helen, the most beautiful woman in the world. She will grow up to be the cause of the Trojan War and – indirectly – the deaths of many warriors, both Greek and Trojan. The Irish poet W.B. Yeats hints at this in two lines from his poem 'Leda and the Swan', which Camille Paglia has called 'the greatest poem of the twentieth century':

> *A shudder in the loins engenders there*
> *The broken wall, the burning roof*
> *and tower*
> *And Agamemnon dead.*

❧

But when the sun had taken his stand at the top of the sky, the Father of the Gods held out his golden scales. He put two portions of death upon them, one side for the Trojans, the other for the Greeks. When he lifted the scales by their middle, the portion of the Greeks sank down. So Zeus thundered loudly and from Ida he threw a sizzling bolt at the army of the Greeks.
Iliad 8.68ff.

❧

THE SOFTER SIDE OF ZEUS:

The earliest literary account in the *Homeric Hymn to Cronides* (Cronides meaning 'son of Cronus', that is, Zeus) praises him as the lord of all who whispers words of wisdom to Themis (goddess of law and order). In Homer's *Iliad*, Zeus is the beleaguered head of the family trying to keep the peace between the gods who support the Trojans and those who support the Greeks. In one of Aesop's Fables dating from the 1ˢᵗ century CE, Zeus creates man from clay with the help of Prometheus, one of the 'good' Titans. He also patiently hears complaints from a number of newly created animals who are unhappy with what he's given them.

Yes, Zeus can be just. The mythical Greek hero Odysseus says, 'May Zeus the god of suppliants make them pay, for he observes all men and he punishes those that sin' (*Odyssey* 13.213).

∼

Zeus, Delighting in Thunder,
is with those who seek his protection…
Odyssey 7.165

∼

FUN FACTS ABOUT ZEUS:

- Some of his most famous children include Apollo, Artemis, Ares, Athena, Dionysus, Heracles, Hebe, Minos of Crete, Persephone, Perseus and Polydeuces (Pollux), but not Castor (see page 152). He also fathered the nine Muses and the three Graces.
- The word 'numinous' (meaning blessed or awe-inspiring) comes from the Latin word *numen*, 'a nodding of the head', because Zeus has looked at the place and nodded his divine approval. For this reason, *numen* came to mean a divine presence.
- On film, the role of Zeus has been played by many actors, including Laurence Olivier, Liam Neeson, Sean Bean, Lance Reddick and Arnold Schwarzenegger, the last in a 2022 BMW commercial.
- In 2022, Irish folk singer Hozier wrote a song called 'Swan Upon Leda' about the experience of women all over the world who suffer oppression and rape.

'I am the most powerful
of all the gods.'
Iliad 8.19

A man loved by Zeus
is worth entire armies.
Iliad 9.116–17

Bronze statuette of Jupiter (Zeus) 1ˢᵗ–2ⁿᵈ century CE, British Museum

HERA

(ROMAN JUNO)
'Queen of the Gods'
The archetypal JEALOUS WIFE

ORIGIN STORY: She was one of the children of Rhea and Cronus. Like most of her siblings, she was swallowed by her father shortly after her birth, then 'resurrected' when Rhea and Zeus made Cronus vomit up the ones he had swallowed. She married her brother Zeus with whom she had a tempestuous relationship.

JOB DESCRIPTION: to help women in childbirth and to get revenge on Zeus by tormenting his illegitimate children by other women.

GODDESS OF: childbirth, marriage, women, family, lawful marriage, wronged wives.

SIGNIFICANT OTHERS: her husband Zeus, to whom she is faithful, and her children Ares, Hephaestus, Hebe and, in some accounts, Eileithyia, a goddess of childbirth.

APPEARANCE: Hera is often shown seated on her throne. One of her defining attributes is a sceptre, which is more like a long staff, often with a twisty design and sometimes with a lotus on top. She almost always wears a crown, sometimes a diadem and sometimes a *polos* (a cylindrical crown). All these show her power as queen of the gods.

EPITHETS: Ox-eyed, Unbulled (i.e. Virgin), Yoking-goddess (i.e. of Marriage) and so on.

≈

Zeus:
'But as for Hera, I'm not as furious with her. I know that she always interferes with my plans.'
Iliad 8.407ff.

≈

THE CATTLE CONNECTION

Ancient Greece was a culture based on sheep, goats and especially cattle. To own cattle, or even a single cow, made you rich. The greatest sacrifice you could make to a god was a bull or cow. Once you start looking for cattle in the myths, you see them everywhere. The first thing baby Hermes does is steal the cattle of Apollo. Prometheus taught humans how to wrap cattle bones in fragrant fat as an offering to the gods, so that people could keep the meat for themselves. Odysseus got in deep trouble for stealing the Cattle of the Sun. Zeus turned the beautiful Io into a heifer to hide her from Hera. He himself became a bull to abduct Europa. And Hera, queen of the gods, is described as 'unbulled', 'yoking-goddess' and 'ox-eyed' (a compliment).

ANIMAL & PLANT ASSOCIATIONS: heifer (female cow), lion, cuckoo, peacock, gadfly, pomegranate (a symbol of fertility).

WHERE TO FIND HER: Hera as Roman Juno often shares a space with Jupiter and Minerva as the Capitoline Triad. But there are two impressive Doric temples of Hera at Paestum, not far from Pompeii. The oldest one, built in 550 BCE, was used in the 1963 film *Jason and the Argonauts* for the story of Phineas and the Harpies.

SOME OF HER BEST-KNOWN MYTHS: Most often identified by her relationship with her philandering husband Zeus, many of her best exploits centre around trying to catch her husband in acts of infidelity or making life hard for his illegitimate children. She was cruel to the female Titan Leto, and tried to prevent her from giving birth to Apollo and Artemis. She delayed the birth of Heracles, tried to kill him by dropping snakes into his cot and tormented him during his life. She hunted down a nymph named Io, whom Zeus hastily turned into a cow. Hera then drove Io the cow mad by the bites of a gadfly.

As Roman Juno, her fury opens the epic Latin poem the *Aeneid*, when the poet Virgil writes, 'On land and sea, Aeneas was badly battered by forces from above, because of cruel Juno's unforgiving wrath' (*Aeneid* 1.3–4).

THE SOFTER SIDE OF HERA:

Hera can be charming when she wants to and is sometimes seen as a protector of married women and those in childbirth. Digging deeper into many of the myths, we see that Hera's ultimate approval is needed for the offspring of Zeus – Heracles, Dionysus, Hephaestus – to be accepted into the family of Mount Olympus. In Etruscan lore, she even suckles the adult Hercle (Heracles) to give him immortality.

GREEK MYTHS VS OVIDIAN MYTHS

Some Greek myths have come down to us by means of only one author. For example, the story of Antigone seems to have been invented by Sophocles (see page 173) and that of Cupid and Psyche (see page 112) is only told by Apuleius in his book The Golden Ass. The Roman poet Ovid also gives us some of our most memorable versions because he was a genius at writing memorable imagery: Arachne becoming a spider, Daphne transforming into a laurel tree, Actaeon morphing into a deer and being devoured by his own hounds.

When Jupiter's lover Alcmene was trying to give birth to a giant baby who would be Hercules (the Roman version of Heracles), Juno caused her to labour for seven days. She asked a goddess of childbirth to sit on an altar outside the bedroom with crossed legs and folded hands, thus shutting Alcmene's womb. The poor mother screamed with pain until a clever maid noticed a figure in a strange position on the altar. 'All is well!' she cried. 'Alcmene has delivered a bouncing boy!' Juno's minion jumped up, and the moment she uncrossed her legs and untwined her fingers, Hercules was finally born.

☞ Painted terracotta figurine of Juno (Hera), 4ᵗʰ centruy BCE, Villa Giulia Etruscan Museum, Rome

GREEK VASES

Many Greek vases are true masterpieces. Today, potters struggle to make pots as light, well balanced, silkily glazed and superbly decorated, even with modern technology. Vases are a window into the world and minds of the ancients. Figures shown on the vases range from the greatest gods to naked enslaved field workers beating olive trees to release their fruit. The faces often show subtle expressions: look out for eye contact, as when Athena takes the toddler Erechtheus from Gaia (see page 98). Observe the gentle smile and expression of tenderness on Achilles' face as he concentrates on bandaging Patroclus' wounded arm. Patroclus bares his teeth in pain and turns his head away, so as not to let Achilles see his discomfort (see page 122).

Emotions are also revealed in stock gestures. The hand to the head in women is an expression of grief and mourning. The hand extended palm up is a gesture asking for mercy. A god or satyr with grasping hand extended and pursuing a woman or nymph is after the obvious thing. And when on many vases Paris leads Helen off to Troy, he grasps her wrist rather than her hand in a gesture which is not quite the same as the hand-holding on many marriage vases. Generally, black-figure vases (where incised black glaze makes the figure) are older than red-figure (where the natural red clay makes the figure, with added touches of black for details).

FUN FACTS ABOUT HERA:

- She gives some horses the ability to speak in *Iliad* 19.407.
- According to Hesiod, Hera raised a lion to terrorize an area called Nemea (*Theogony* 327ff.). Its skin was impervious to weapons so Heracles strangled it as the first of his 'twelve tasks'. He then used its own sharp claws to skin it and make it into his iconic lion-head cape that protected him.
- When Zeus gives Hera the infant Heracles to suckle in order to make him immortal, the moment she discovers the baby is Heracles she thrusts him away. The milk that spurts from her breast sprays across the heavens to form the Milky Way.

~

Hera to Zeus:
'I am a god like you, with the same parents. In fact, I am the eldest child of our devious father Cronus.'
Iliad 4.58ff.

~

- When I was studying at Cambridge in the late 1970s, the Classics Library was in the same building as a gallery full of life-sized plaster casts of many Greek gods and goddesses. One day I was heading through the cast gallery to the ladies' room, walking briskly in my new cowboy boots. Suddenly, my heel slipped on the freshly waxed floor and I crashed to the ground, accidentally knocking one of the pale-blue bases with a plaster bust of Hera on top. Time seemed to slow down as I watched the base rock one way while the bust rocked the other. I had a terrifying vision of all the casts going down like dominoes. In the end, only the Hera crashed to the floor. Ashen-faced, I reported the accident. Professor Hugh Plummer and others came rushing. 'It can be fixed,' they reassured me. 'If you had to break one cast,' wheezed Professor Plummer, 'the Farnese Hera was the best choice.'
- In the 1963 film *Jason and the Argonauts*, Hera is played sympathetically by Honor Blackman, better known as Pussy Galore in the 1964 Bond film *Goldfinger*.
- In the post-#MeToo era, the queen of the gods has often been shown as a sympathetic character.

HEPHAESTUS

(ROMAN VULCAN)
'God of the Forge'
The archetypal UNDERESTIMATED MISFIT

ORIGIN STORY: According to some accounts, Hephaestus is the son of Zeus and Hera, but in other versions Hera gave birth to him on her own (because goddesses can do that). He was either born lame, or he was disabled after being tossed off Mount Olympus because he was so ugly. Either way, the young god was raised by the sea nymph Thetis in an underwater grotto, possibly near the island of Lemnos. When grown, he organized his return to Olympus by sending his mother a beautifully crafted throne that held her fast. He vowed he would only release her if the gods gave him Aphrodite as a wife and received him back among them. A popular scene on Greek vases is the return of Hephaestus to Olympus, where he rides a mule, accompanied by Dionysus. On one vase he is even shown returning in a winged chariot, as if it were a prototype wheelchair.

JOB DESCRIPTION: blacksmith, inventor, armourer, cupbearer to the gods, occasional court jester, pyromaniac, cuckold.

GOD OF: fire, volcanoes, metallurgy, invention, those with disabilities, craftsmen, blacksmiths, armourers, bakers, potters and anyone who works with fire.

SIGNIFICANT OTHERS: Hephaestus was unhappily married to Aphrodite. He also loved Aglaia, Athena (who spurned him) and others. He had a surprising number of offspring.

APPEARANCE: Hephaestus is the only Olympian who works. Recognize him by his metalworking tools, usually tongs and pincers. Sometimes he is shown with feet that are small or twisted. His usual costume is the *exomis* (a one-shouldered sleeveless tunic), a conical hat called a *petasos* and his tongs or hammer. Although he is often described as hairy, barrel-chested and monstrous, he is sometimes shown on vases as a handsome bridegroom riding a mule to Olympus to be married to the goddess of love.

EPITHETS: Very Famous Limping God, Lame, Shrivelled-legged, Club-footed, Shrewd, Inventive, Clever Craftsman, Coppersmith, Sooty, Glorious.

ANIMAL & PLANT ASSOCIATIONS: The special animal of Hephaestus is the mule (or donkey) that carries him up to Olympus to marry Aphrodite.

WHERE TO FIND HIM: the well-preserved Doric Temple of Hephaestus in the Athenian agora (marketplace), now full of plants, feral cats and tortoises. He is also associated with the island of Lemnos, where the airport is named after him.

ONE OF HIS BEST-KNOWN MYTHS: Having won Aphrodite as his wife, Hephaestus was humiliated to discover she was having an affair with his brother Ares, god of war. So he crafted an almost invisible metal net and dropped it on them the next time they were making love. He then invited the gods to come and see the disgraced couple. Out of modesty the goddesses refused, but the male gods all crowded into the room and had a good laugh.

THE SOFTER SIDE OF HEPHAESTUS: Near the end of the first chapter of the *Iliad*, Hephaestus arouses 'unquenchable laughter' at a banquet of the gods on Olympus as he puffs up and down, serving wine. His parents, Zeus and Hera, have been fighting but the laughter breaks the tension. Was Hephaestus consciously hamming it up to defuse a potentially explosive argument between Hera and Zeus? I suspect so. This is a recurring theme: often mocked at first, the smith god eventually wins people over by his wit, persistence and special skills.

∽

'I am weak. If only I had not been born.'
Odyssey 8.311ff.

∽

☞ Hephaestus and winged chariot on a drinking
cup *c.*525 BCE, once in Berlin, now lost

HESIOD VS RODDENBERRY

In *Works and Days*, written in the 7th century BCE, Hesiod proposed the theory that humankind has been deteriorating. Long ago there was a Golden Age, followed by a Silver Age and
a Bronze Age, each age worse than the previous one. The current age was the worst of all. In
the 1960s, Gene Roddenberry's sci-fi TV show *Star Trek* proposed the opposite: people are
evolving into something better. By the 24th century, the time Captain James T. Kirk and his
pals are flying around in the Starship *Enterprise*, humanity has become something noble and
good. But, as any classicist will tell you, humanity has not changed one jot.

THE FOUR HUMOURS

In Greek and Roman times, there was a deep-seated belief that the world was made of four different elements: Fire, Air, Earth and Water. These elements corresponded to the seasons and types of food and drink. Humans contained liquid versions of these elements. The Latin word for 'liquid' is *umor*, hence the term 'the Four Humours'.

Everyone had more of one element than the others, determining your temperament. Fire equated with yellow bile or choler and made you choleric or hot-tempered. Water could be found in phlegm and made you phlegmatic or easy-going. Earth went with black bile, and if you had too much, you were melancholic. Sanguine people were often cheerful and had too much blood or *sanguis*. Their element was Air.

Hippocrates, Galen and many other ancient doctors believed that a balanced combination of the four humours kept the body in good health. If you got out of balance, you could become sick. Various remedies were prescribed to get you back in balance, for example a special diet or bloodletting. This deep-seated, pervasive belief, alien to us now, can be seen in those of the gods and goddesses who represent primal elements.

~

Hephaestus speaking of Aphrodite:
'With her shameless puppy-dog eyes, the daughter of Zeus is beautiful but has no self-control.'
Odyssey 8.319

~

FUN FACTS ABOUT HEPHAESTUS:

᪐ In the Gigantomachy (the battle of gods and giants, see page 103), Hephaestus fights with molten iron and burning coals flung from his tongs.

᪐ In the Trojan War, Hephaestus uses his fire to make the river Scamander boil.

᪐ Hephaestus is credited with inventing the first robots: three-legged braziers that could walk around, beautiful female servants made of gold, a golden watchdog and the bronze bodyguard Talos (see page 190). He crafted many other things, including the winged sandals and cap of Hermes, the chain that bound Prometheus and even Aphrodite's magical girdle. Perhaps most famously, he made new armour for Achilles, including a splendid shield that Homer takes a hundred lines to describe (*Iliad* 18.478–608).

᪐ After his wife Aphrodite slept with Ares, she gave birth to Harmonia. Hephaestus bided his time and on Harmonia's wedding day he gave her a necklace with a curse attached. Her descendants were duly miserable and included Oedipus, who murdered his father and married his own mother.

᪐ Potters, bakers and blacksmiths often put a small statuette of Hephaestus/Vulcan near their kiln, oven or furnace in order to protect against fire.

᪐ The name Hephaestus can be used to stand in for fire, as in *Iliad* 2.426. This is called metonymy.

᪐ The god's lameness may reflect the fact that many ancient blacksmiths used arsenic for smelting copper – breathing the fumes can, in extreme cases, cause weakness in one or both legs.

᪐ The Hephaestus Smart Wheelchair System (components that clinicians and wheelchair manufacturers could attach to standard power wheelchairs to make them 'smart wheelchairs') was proposed in the early 2000s.

᪐ In my children's book *The Secrets of Vesuvius*, I introduce a character named Vulcan who is a clubfoot blacksmith. My story contains lots of references to the god of smiths and to some of the myths about him. There is a dramatic scene during one of his festivals, the Vulcanalia, which occurred every year on 23 August, the day before one of the proposed dates for the eruption of Vesuvius.

᪐ In the popular video game *Assassin's Creed Odyssey*, players must find the workshop of Hephaestus. The workshop is accessed via a cleft in a mountain.

᪐ In the *Percy Jackson and the Olympians* TV series, Hephaestus is played by disabled actor Timothy Omundson.

ATHENA

(ROMAN MINERVA)
'Goddess of Wisdom'
The archetypal CAREER WOMAN

ORIGIN STORY: Zeus made love to Metis, a goddess of cunning intelligence (which is what *metis* means). When she became pregnant, he swallowed her, fearing her offspring might usurp him. Not long afterwards he had a splitting headache and begged his son Hephaestus to give his head a tap with an axe. Hephaestus obliged by cracking open his father's head and out popped Athena, fully armed. This scene is popular on vases made in Athens, Athena's special city.

JOB DESCRIPTION: mentor to heroes, planner, strategist, warrior, inventor, weaver, foster mother.

GODDESS OF: Athenians, craftsmen and craftswomen, weavers, potters, orators, inventors, agriculture and anything to do with olive production.

SIGNIFICANT OTHERS: Athena remained a virgin, although she had a fondness for various heroes such as Odysseus and Heracles. The closest she comes to having a child is after wiping the semen of the excited Hephaestus from her thigh (see page 33). Erechtheus is born from the earth and becomes the first ruler of Athens.

APPEARANCE: Athena is shown as tall and calm, with a long robe, spear, helmet pushed back to show her face and, most importantly, an aegis (see page 32). The Greek word used to describe her eyes – *glaucopis* – can mean 'grey-eyed' or possibly 'owl-eyed'.

EPITHETS: Grey-eyed, Aegis-Bearer, Virgin, Of the City, She Who Fights in Front (Promachos), Tireless, Skilled, Tritogenia, and so on. In her home town of Athens, she is Athena Ergane ('female worker') and is the patroness of potters.

ANIMAL & PLANT ASSOCIATIONS: Athena likes owls, snakes and spiders, and her special plant is the olive tree.

WHERE TO FIND HER: the Parthenon in Athens, the city named after her. Built atop the Acropolis, the tallest part of Athens, it was burned by the Persians in 490 BCE. It was rebuilt by the statesman Pericles in the 440s and 430s. The temple was designed by Ictinus, a genius of architecture. The gold-and-ivory statue inside the temple was made by Pheidias, possibly the greatest sculptor of all time. Another, even bigger bronze statue of Athena stood in the open air and towered over the Parthenon on top of the Acropolis; one of the first things approaching travellers saw was the glint of light on the tip of her spear.

〜

Athena to Odysseus:
'I am a goddess. I have protected you during your many trials.'
Odyssey 20.47ff.

〜

WHAT IS AN AEGIS?

The aegis (pronounced EE-jiss) is a strange garment. A kind of powerful protective poncho made variously of goatskin (the meaning of the Greek word *aigis*), snake-skin or gold metal, it can be worn as a cape, a bib or even a shield. Hephaestus made it 'for Zeus to carry, for putting men to flight' (*Iliad* 15.310ff.). Zeus loans it out to his children, especially Athena, who often wears it on vases. In *Iliad* 5.732ff., Homer tells how she took off the soft tunic she herself had woven and put on her father's tunic and over it the fringed aegis with 'the head of the terrible monster, the gorgon' as she prepares to go to battle.

The *gorgoneion* (head of Medusa) and scary snakes on the aegis are apotropaic – that is, they turn away evil. The material of the aegis can change over time and place; so, too, the colour. It is often gold or bright when Athena is in a good mood but dark if she is angry. Although it was originally made for Zeus who is called 'Aegis-Bearer', Athena is the one who wears it most often. However, in *Iliad* 24.20, Apollo uses it to preserve Hector's body, and even Aphrodite has been spotted wearing it on vases.

ONE OF HER BEST-KNOWN MYTHS:
the story of Arachne. In a tale told by the
Roman poet Ovid, a girl named Arachne
boasts that she is a better weaver than
Minerva (Athena). Disguising herself
as an old woman, Minerva asks the girl
if this is true. The girl maintains her
position, even when Minerva reveals
herself. They have a contest. Arachne
wins, Minerva is furious and turns her
into a spider as punishment for her hubris.

THE SOFTER SIDE OF ATHENA:
Although she is skilled at weaving and
pottery, Athena is not a homemaker. She
never marries (the Greek word for wife,
damar, means 'a tamed thing') but wants
to be active in the world of men, taking
part in politics, science and machinations.
She is a generous mentor to several heroes,
especially Heracles, Odysseus, Patroclus
and Perseus. She is most sympathetic as the
mother of Erechtheus. How did the virgin
goddess become a mother? Hephaestus
approached her in an amorous mood,
and Athena recoiled in disgust so that his
seed spilled on her thigh. She wiped it off
with a piece of wool and threw it on the
ground. Gaia (Earth) acted as surrogate
mother and gave birth to a child born of
Hephaestus' semen and Athena's wool. A
popular scene on Athenian vases shows
Athena warmly receiving baby Erechtheus
from Gaia (see page 98).

Somewhat confusingly also known
as Erichthonius, Erechtheus is sometimes
shown with snake legs or even as a snake,
a creature believed to live in the ground.
He grows up to be the first ruler of
Athens, city of Athena.

WHAT IS HUBRIS?

Although its original Greek meaning
was violence or insolence, the word came
to mean 'overweening' (defiant) pride,
especially in dealings with the gods. In
myths and tragedies, any demonstration
of hubris is inevitably punished by spec-
tacular disaster.

Do not even think about comparing
yourself to the gods. And if you are a girl
in a Greek myth and an old woman comes
to give you advice, beware. Chances are it
is a goddess in disguise, testing your piety
and humility.

~

Cloud-gathering Zeus smiled.
'Cheer up, Tritogenia, dear child, and
don't take my shouting to heart; I never
want to upset you.'
Iliad 8.38

~

Athena came towards him disguised as a young
shepherd with skin as soft as a prince's. She wore a
cloak of fine wool over her shoulders and sandals on
her tender feet. And she held a javelin.

Odyssey 13.221ff.

Athena gives the *harpe* (sickle) to Perseus on a vase *c.*370 BCE, British Museum

FUN FACTS ABOUT ATHENA:

ॐ She and Poseidon both wanted a certain city in a part of Greece called Attica. They went up to a tall rock there called an acropolis. Poseidon struck the top of the rock with his trident and a saltwater spring appeared. Athena produced an olive tree, a source of food, light, warmth, medicine, beautifying balm and, used as an anointing oil, even supernatural blessing. Athena won the contest and the city was called Athens after her. The contest was depicted on the west pediment of the Parthenon, of which only fragments remain.

ॐ The great temple to her on the Acropolis of Athens is called the Parthenon, because *parthenos* means 'virgin' and Athena was the virgin goddess.

ॐ The centrepiece of the Parthenon's east pediment (in the British Museum at the time of writing) showed the birth of Athena. Sadly, those central figures are lost.

ॐ Today, you can see a life-sized version of the Parthenon in Nashville, Tennessee – the 'Athens of the South'. Now serving as Nashville's art museum, it contains a replica of Pheidias' gold-and-ivory statue of Athena.

ॐ The monumental bronze statue of Athena Promachos that stood next to the Parthenon is brilliantly depicted in the computer game *Assassin's Creed Odyssey*, where the player's avatar can climb to the top of her helmet for a breathtaking view of ancient Athens.

ॐ Because she bore the mysterious epithet Tritogenia (possibly meaning 'thrice-born'), the Pythagoreans gave the name 'Athena' to the equilateral triangle.

～

Grey-eyed Athena wore the precious aegis, ageless and immortal, with its hundred fluttering gold tassels, each worth more than a hundred oxen.
Iliad 2.446ff.

～

APHRODITE

(ROMAN VENUS)
'Goddess of Love'
The archetypal SEX GODDESS

ORIGIN STORY: Aphrodite is one of the oldest immortals, having emerged from the foam of the severed genitals of the sky god Uranus (see page 106) after they had fallen into the sea in a foamy froth (Aphrodite means 'foam-born'). However, Homer assigns her Zeus and Dione (a sea goddess) as parents in the *Iliad*, perhaps to emphasize the familial feel of the epic.

JOB DESCRIPTION: She causes people to desire one another passionately. She also protects sailors at sea.

GOD OF: love, erotic passion, beauty, luxury, femininity, lovers, sailors, Pompeii.

SIGNIFICANT OTHERS: Her official husband was Hephaestus by arranged marriage. Being the goddess of love, she has several affairs: Ares, Hermes, Dionysus, Poseidon, Phaethon, Boutes, Adonis and Anchises.

APPEARANCE: That she is beautiful almost goes without saying. From her we get an idea of the ideal beauty of each period. Shown clothed in the oldest representations of her, she later becomes the first of the goddesses to shed her clothes and appear nude or semi-nude. She is often depicted bathing, and you can recognize her by her tiara, girdle (see page 38) and sandals. Her Roman counterpart, Venus, accessorizes with a shell or mirror. She is often accompanied by Eros or Cupid(s).

EPITHETS: Cyprus, Cyprian, Of Paphos, Foam-born, Daughter of Zeus, Daughter of Dione (from another version of her birth), Laughter-loving, Golden, Divine, Mother of Desire, Richly Garlanded, Of the Sea, Of the Harbour, Of the Stranger, Well-girdled and so on.

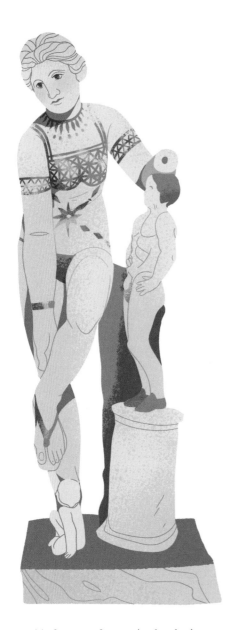

GIRDLE OR WONDERBRA?

In Homer's *Iliad*, one of our oldest sources, Aphrodite has a garment that she loans to Hera, who wants to seduce Zeus and make herself look more attractive. The words *himas* (leather strap, rope) and *kestos* (embroidered thing) are both used in the passage. Aphrodite's garment is often translated as 'belt' or 'girdle'. Girdle makes me think of adverts from the 1960s, when women still wore girdles. Would the modern version be Spanx?

Nobody is quite sure what the ancient garment was, although there is a small marble statue from Pompeii showing Venus wearing a painted gold bikini. So maybe it was a kind of ancient version of the Wonderbra of the 1990s, made famous by the 'Hello Boys' billboards. Whatever it was, it never failed to work.

Marble figurine of Venus (Aphrodite),
1ˢᵗ century BCE–1ˢᵗ century CE, from
Pompeii, now in Naples

~

Muse, tell me about very golden
Aphrodite from Cyprus...
Homeric Hymn
to Aphrodite, 1

~

ANIMAL & PLANT ASSOCIATIONS:
apple, myrtle, rose, poppy, dove,
sparrow, hare.

WHERE TO FIND HER: Aphrodite is
usually associated with Paphos, a town
on the isle of Cyprus where she is said to
have come ashore. In another account,
she comes ashore on the Greek island of
Cythera, where her earliest temple was,
according to the historian Herodotus.
This was the Temple of Aphrodite
Ourania (daughter of Uranus). Aphrodite
was also famous at Cnidus, a now-deserted
site on the coast of Turkey, thanks to the
first shocking but hugely successful nude
statue of her on display there.

Later, in her Roman guise as Venus,
she was the patron goddess of Pompeii,
Venus Pompeiana. Her temple in Pompeii
was badly damaged by an earthquake and
was still undergoing repairs when it was
buried by the ash and pumice of Vesuvius
17 years later.

ONE OF HER BEST-KNOWN MYTHS:
Eris, the goddess of strife, was not
invited to the wedding of a sea nymph
named Thetis and a mortal man named
Peleus (see page 121). In revenge, she
showed up at the wedding feast and
tossed in a golden apple inscribed 'To
the Most Beautiful'. Three goddesses
immediately claimed the prize: Hera,

Athena and Aphrodite. They asked Zeus
to judge, but he passed the task along
to a handsome shepherd named Paris,
who was secretly a Trojan prince. This is
famously called the Judgement of Paris.
Hera offered Paris power if he would
choose her. Athena offered him wisdom.
But Aphrodite won the prize by offering
him possession of the most beautiful
woman in the world, Helen of Sparta.
The only problem was that Helen was
already married to Menelaus, king of
Sparta. When Paris ran off with her it
sparked the ten-year-long Trojan War.

⟳

Deathless Aphrodite
on your jewelled throne,
daughter of Zeus,
weaver of deception,
do not overwhelm
my courage with
desire and distress,
I beg you, O goddess.
Sappho, Ode to Aphrodite, 1ff.

⟳

THE SOFTER SIDE OF APHRODITE: In the ancient *Homeric Hymn to Aphrodite*, she is said to have power over all the gods except for the three virgin goddesses Athena, Artemis and Hestia. In order to humble Aphrodite, Zeus causes her to fall in love with a handsome shepherd named Anchises and she has a son by him, Aeneas. During the Trojan War, she sticks close to her son in order to help him, but she is no warrior; on one occasion she is wounded in the hand by Diomedes and has to retreat in tears.

Later, when Aeneas flees burning Troy, he must carry his lame father on his back, the once-handsome shepherd Aphrodite loved. Aeneas eventually founds a new Troy in Italy, near the place that will one day become Rome. When Julius Caesar claimed Aeneas as his ancestor it meant that he also counted Aphrodite, or Venus as he called her, his ancestress. For this reason she is known as *genetrix* ('ancestress') of the Romans.

Terracotta figurine of Venus rising from water, 1st century CE, British Museum

VENUS PUDICA

The word *pudica* is Latin for 'chaste', 'ashamed' and 'modest'. It comes from the root *pudeo*, 'to make ashamed or feel shame'. The word *pudenda* (visible genitals) literally means 'causing shame'. Venus Pudica is the type of statue of the goddess of love shown nude but holding her hands in front of her breasts and pudenda. Naturally, this has the effect of drawing the viewer's attention to precisely those parts.

FUN FACTS ABOUT APHRODITE:

๑๏ She often works in conjunction with her son Eros whose arrows arouse love. Eros can be a lone adolescent or multiple cupids, who act like naughty toddlers in Roman art.

๑๏ Sometimes Aphrodite wields a slipper as an erotic weapon to defend herself against randy satyrs and fauns.

๑๏ The name Aphrodite can be used as a metonym for the act of love (for example, *Odyssey* 22.444).

๑๏ In a story told by the Roman poet Ovid, Venus loved a beautiful youth named Adonis. When he was gored to death by a boar, she turned his blood into an anemone flower (Ovid, *Metamorphoses* 10.519–53).

๑๏ She is often depicted in activities to do with the bath: undressing, bathing, washing her hair and getting dressed again. These are all excuses to show her nude.

๑๏ However, in her localized guise as Venus Pompeiana, patron goddess of the port of Pompeii, she appears fully clothed with a staff, crown and rudder. In nearby Naples, she is also fully clothed in her function as Aphrodite Sosandra ('Who Saves Men').

๑๏ Aphrodite/Venus is a powerful ever-present theme in popular culture, especially featuring in Roman times, the Renaissance and the modern period. Just as the Aphrodite of Praxiteles was ground-breaking in showing her nudity in the mid-4th century BCE, so Sandro Botticelli's *Birth of Venus* was ground-breaking in the late 15th century, again for showing nudity. For many centuries before, nobody had dared show a female nude of a non-biblical character. Botticelli's painting of Venus has become as iconic today as the Aphrodite of Cnidus was in ancient times.

๑๏ In the Bond film *Dr. No* (1962), Ursula Andress as Honey Ryder memorably emerges from the sea like Aphrodite.

~

Zeus called Golden Aphrodite to himself. 'The art of war is not for you, dear child. Attend to your own charming skills, those of the honeymoon night. Leave warfare to swift Ares and Athena.'

Iliad 5.427ff.

~

POSEIDON

(ROMAN NEPTUNE)
'King of the Sea'
The archetypal RESENTFUL BROTHER

ORIGIN STORY: In most versions of his origin, Poseidon was swallowed by Cronus soon after birth, along with his siblings Hades, Hestia, Demeter and Hera. But one version says he was replaced by a colt (instead of a rock, like Zeus) and spirited away to the island of Rhodes. When Cronus was deposed, his three sons shook lots in a helmet to see who would get the different parts of the world (Earth being common to all). Zeus received the most desirable residence, the sky, Hades got the underworld and Poseidon, the sea. Although Poseidon looks like Zeus, he is not as strong as his older brother and he is more volatile.

JOB DESCRIPTION: He rules the waves, causes earthquakes, stirs up storms, makes life hard for Odysseus and other sailors, and grumbles about Zeus.

GOD OF: oceans, earthquakes, horses, fish, sea monsters, fishermen, sponge divers and sailors...unless he has a grudge against them.

SIGNIFICANT OTHERS: Almost as randy as his brother Zeus, Poseidon has many lovers apart from his wife Amphitrite: Aethra, Alcyone, Alope, Amymone, Caenis, Demeter, Larissa, Medusa,

Theophane, Tyro. His offspring include Bellerophon, Charybdis, Polyphemus, Procrustes and Theseus.

APPEARANCE: black beard and long black hair (sometimes delightfully dark blue or blue-green). From his earliest depictions in literature and art, he drives a chariot over the waves. In Homer, the horses are so skilled that the bronze chariot axle barely gets wet. He often holds a trident, used by fishermen for spearing underwater prey. Sometimes he is accompanied by his wife, Amphitrite. He accessorizes with sea nymphs, fish, dolphins, horses and the occasional hippocamp (imagine the front of a horse ending in a muscular, slippery, curvy fish tail). One of his weapons (apart from his trident) is the island of Nisyros, which he uses as a boulder in the Gigantomachy (see page 103).

(see page 103)

EPITHETS: Earth-shaker, Protector of Ships, Tamer of Horses, Of the High Sea, Of the Open Sea, Abounding in Waves, Sea-sounding, Earth-holding and so on.

HOW THE GREEKS USED COLOUR

Poseidon's 'blue hair' makes me recall the DC comics of my youth, when Superman's black hair was inked with dark-blue highlights. But it seems the Greeks used words for colour in a slightly different way than we do, a more synaesthetic way, sometimes attaching the emotional associations of objects to their colour.

The most famous example is Homer's 'wine-dark' sea. Obviously, the sea is not deep red or even the colour of some new wines so dark they are almost black. But wine can make you unsteady, queasy and out of control, just like the sea. The word *xanthus* means 'tawny' (like a lion) or 'yellow' (like bile that causes a hot temper) and is often used to describe angry people. The word *kyanos* (literally 'cyan' or 'blue') was sometimes applied to the sea so it is perfect for Poseidon's blue-black hair.

COLOURS & THEIR MEANINGS

Glaukos – grey, silver, greenish-grey, gleaming (like an olive leaf)

Ioeides – violet, deep-blue, purple (like the *ion*, or violet flower)

Khruseos – golden, golden-yellow, bright (like gold)

Krokeos – saffron-yellow, orange, expensive (like cloth dyed with crocus stigmas)

Kyanos – dark, dark blue (of enamel), angry, fertile (like dark earth)

Melas – black, murky, malignant, dark (like the black cloud of grief)

Oinops – literally 'wine-faced', wine-red, reddish (like an ox's face)

Pyrrhos – 'tawny red' of a flame, the colour of an egg yolk, ginger (like hair)

Xanthos – yellow, tawny, reddish-brown, chestnut or bay (horses)

ANIMAL & PLANT ASSOCIATIONS:
Although seaweed (or kelp) seems the
obvious plant of choice for Poseidon,
pine and wild celery were used as
crowns in the games held in his honour.
His animals were dolphins, fish, sea
monsters, bulls and especially horses.

WHERE TO FIND HIM: The beautiful
Doric Temple of Poseidon at Cape
Sounion is a must-see sight in Greece.
Go at the right time for sunset or
moonrise, and look out for the famous
graffiti by Lord Byron (or at least his
name) carved into the limestone. The
section with Byron's name is now roped
off, so take your binoculars.

ONE OF HIS BEST-KNOWN MYTHS:
In Homer's *Iliad*, Poseidon recounts
how he built the walls of Troy after
he and Apollo had conspired against
Zeus. Their bid for power failed and,
as punishment, Zeus assigned them
to work for the then king of Troy,
Laomedon, at workers' wages. Apollo
had to herd cattle and Poseidon had
to build the walls of the citadel. When
Laomedon refused to pay the gods for
their work as agreed, Poseidon sent a sea
monster to ravage the land around Troy.
A few generations later, the Greeks tore
down the sea god's great wall. In revenge,
angry Poseidon and Apollo destroyed

the Greeks' own sea wall so that no trace
of them would remain at Troy.

THE SOFTER SIDE OF POSEIDON:
There isn't a softer side to Poseidon.
He is a big grumpy-boots. The
Phaeacians were a cheerful race of sailors
with self-driving ships who liked to
help sailors in distress. But Poseidon
became angry at them because they
sailed Odysseus safely home to Ithaca.
When their ship returned to harbour,
Poseidon turned it into stone, as a
constantly visible warning. As a result,
one of their prophets advised them, 'Let's
stop guiding mortal sailors who come
here. And we had better sacrifice twelve
fine bulls to Poseidon, otherwise he
might bury us with a massive mountain'
(*Odyssey* 13.180ff.).

~

'I will not submit to Zeus' will.
Despite his power, let him stay in his own
third. And let him not try to frighten me,
as if I were a coward.'
Iliad 15.194ff.

~

45

FUN FACTS ABOUT POSEIDON:

- Why was Poseidon so strongly associated with earthquakes? Possibly because they are often followed by tsunamis. The Greeks thought of the sea as surrounding and supporting the disk of the earth. If the earth wobbles, it must be the fault of Poseidon the 'Earth-enfolder' (*Iliad* 13.125).

- Poseidon has an ancient and strong association with horses, and is given the epithet *hippios* (Creator of Horses) by Aeschylus and others. After Poseidon slept with Medusa, she conceived the winged horse Pegasus, who was 'born' after Perseus cut off her head.

- When Demeter was wandering the Earth in search of her daughter Persephone, Poseidon desired her and pursued her. She took the form of a mare to elude him, but Poseidon changed himself into a stallion. He caught up with her and their union produced a girl and a horse.

- When Odysseus blinds the Cyclops Polyphemus, who is one of Poseidon's sons, he makes a dangerous enemy. Poseidon throws winds at him, overturns his ships and sends his daughter Scylla to devour the sailors. Only Odysseus survives.

- As Ajax the Lesser made his way home from Troy, Poseidon wrecked his ships but spared the man himself. When Ajax boasted that he had survived the waves 'in spite of the gods', Poseidon furiously struck the rock upon which he sat and drowned him.

- After Poseidon lost the contest to get Athens as his special city, he threw a tantrum and flooded the Attic plain.

- In the Percy Jackson books, Poseidon is the father of Percy (Perseus) Jackson. Every time Percy stands in water or has a drink he gains power.

~

Lord Poseidon Earth-Shaker…saw Odysseus from afar and shook his angry head…'I'll give him his fill of trouble yet!' He gathered his clouds, seized his trident and stirred up the sea. He summoned every wind and told them to blow a tempest.

Odyssey 5.282ff.

~

'Zeus the Earth-shaker may be powerful, but it is preposterous for him to suggest he can beat me, his equal. We are three brothers, born to Cronus by Rhea: Zeus and I and Hades, the Lord of the Dead. The world was divided in three and each of us brothers was given an equal share when lots were cast. I drew the restless sea as my realm forever, and Hades the murky gloom of the underworld, and Zeus the broad sky, and the clouds and the upper air. But the earth and the heights of Olympus were left to us all.'

Iliad 15.185ff.

☞ Poseidon with dolphin and trident
on a vase c.440 BCE, British Museum

HERMES

(ROMAN MERCURY)
'Messenger God'
The archetypal TRICKSTER

ORIGIN STORY: Zeus spotted Maia, the eldest of the Pleiades, and desired her. Nine months later, little Hermes was born, a trickster and inventor from day one. Charmed by a slow-moving tortoise, the inquisitive baby pulled off its legs and head and scooped it out to see what was inside. He then took some sticks of wood and handy cow intestines and made the tortoise shell into a lyre, the first stringed instrument known to gods or men.

Next, he decided to steal some cattle belonging to his older brother Apollo. He cleverly drove them backwards into a cave so anyone tracking them would think they had come out of the cave. To disguise his little footprints, he tied leafy branches to his feet. Hearing Zeus and Apollo approaching to investigate, he jumped back into his cradle, pulled his swaddling clothes up around his ears and pretended to be a helpless baby. They weren't fooled. So he made Zeus laugh with clever stories and charmed Apollo by giving him the lyre.

JOB DESCRIPTION: trickster, messenger and psychopomp (escort to the underworld).

GOD OF: boundaries, thresholds, roads, trade, trickery, messengers, heralds, public speakers, travellers, merchants, thieves, gymnasts, athletes, herdsmen and shepherds.

SIGNIFICANT OTHERS: Hermes never married but loved several goddesses, including Aphrodite and Persephone. He also loved various nymphs, mortal women and a youth named Crocus who was turned into a flower upon his death.

APPEARANCE: On the oldest Greek vases Hermes is bearded, but already by the Classical period he has become beardless and boyish with a handsome face and curly hair. Recognize him on vases and sculptures by his winged sandals, winged *petasos* (flat hat) and especially his *caduceus* (herald's wand). A *chlamys* (short travelling cloak) does little to cover his youthful nakedness. He is obviously in too much of a rush to put on his tunic.

EPITHETS: Son of Maia, Killer of Argus, Escorter of Souls (*psychopompos*), Ram Bearer (*kriophoros*), Crafty (*polytropos*) and so on.

ANIMAL & PLANT ASSOCIATIONS: tortoise, cattle, ram, hawk, hare, cockerel, crocus, arbutus (sometimes known as the strawberry tree.

WHERE TO FIND HIM: The so-called Temple of Mercury at Baiae near Naples was not a temple to Mercury but part of a luxurious bath complex and is well worth a visit. Hermes doesn't have many temples dedicated to him, but statues representing him could be found at a thousand crossroads and boundaries across ancient Greece. These statues are called herms and are border guardians: square pillars with a sculpted head on top and an erect phallus halfway down.

These pillars probably developed from the early practice of piling stones at crossroads and boundaries. The Greek word for 'pile of stones', 'cairn' or 'column' is *herma,* and this may be where Hermes got his name. These herm pillars with head and genitals were apotropaic – that is, they deflected malicious spirits at vulnerable borders, especially doorways and crossroads. This may be primal: some baboons guard their groups by facing outwards with erect phalluses.

∼

Odysseus:
'Hermes of the Golden Wand came to meet me as I was going to the house. He looked like a young man just getting a beard, the most appealing age.'
Odyssey 10.276ff.

∼

ONE OF HIS BEST-KNOWN MYTHS:

The Roman poet Ovid tells of the time Hermes and Zeus disguised themselves to visit a town in Phrygia (now part of modern Turkey) in order to see if its people would exhibit *xenia*, the Greek custom of hospitality. A thousand homes turned them away. Finally, there was only one cottage left, the home of a very poor old couple named Baucis and Philemon. Despite their extreme poverty, they offered the two strangers hospitality and food. Hermes and Zeus punished the heartless inhabitants by drowning them in a flood but rewarded Baucis and Philemon by giving them a good living and turning them into trees at the hour of their death.

About 40 years after Ovid wrote down this story, a Jew named Paul travelled with his friend Barnabas to that same region of Phrygia to proclaim the good news of a new Messiah. The New Testament recounts that when the locals saw them heal a man who had been lame from birth they became very excited and cried, 'The gods have disguised themselves as men and come to visit us. They called Barnabas Zeus and Paul they called Hermes, because he was the chief speaker' (Acts 14.8ff.).

THE SOFTER SIDE OF HERMES:

Hermes can be affable, with a self-deprecating sense of humour. In a fable of Aesop, first recorded around the time of Christ, he saunters into a sculptor's shop disguised as an ordinary mortal. Seeing a statue of Zeus, he asks the sculptor its price. 'One drachma' comes the reply. 'And the statue of Hera?' 'Two drachmas.' Hermes grins. 'And how much is the Hermes?' he asks, certain that *his* image must be worth even more. 'Tell you what,' says the sculptor, 'if you buy the other two, I'll throw that one in for free.'

~

'You crafty creature!'
cried Apollo. 'How were you
able to skin two cows?
You're just a baby!'
Homeric Hymn to Hermes 405–6

~

FUN FACTS ABOUT HERMES:

- Argus was a giant with hundred eyes employed by Hera as a watchman. Hermes, acting as hitman for Zeus, made Argus sleepy with a long story about the invention of panpipes. When all hundred eyes had closed, Hermes cut off the giant's head, winning for himself the epithet Slayer of Argus.

- All the gods can fly (or at least flit) but Hermes is the fastest because daddy Zeus gave him flying shoes and a traveller's hat with wings.

- Like Odysseus, Hermes often gives a false identity with an elaborate fictional backstory when introducing himself. Why tell the truth if you can get away with a tall story?

- Hermes is usually a cheerful helper and rarely vindictive. However, when Pelops kills one of his sons, the messenger god blights the lives of his offspring – Atreus, Menelaus, Agamemnon, Electra and Orestes – with incest, adultery, fratricide, mariticide, matricide, filicide and war.

- Hermes is often shown as the Kriophorus, the ram bearer. Our earliest depictions of Jesus are as a beardless Good Shepherd, and sometimes we cannot be sure which of the two we are looking at, Hermes or Jesus.

- In Roman Britain, Mercury was associated with cockerels, possibly because it feels like their cacophonous crowing could wake you from death as well as sleep. Or is it because you could win a lot betting on cockerel fights? The wand (*caduceus*) of Hermes, the god of profit, is often shown beside money bags and a victorious cockerel.

- The earliest version of his *caduceus* is a stick with two circles on top (sometimes the top circle has a gap), then the circles become two snakes coiling around the staff and finally wings are added somewhere near the top. The snakes cause it to be confused with the staff of Asclepius, which had only one snake, and thus Hermes' wand became a symbol of medicine in the United States.

- The Romantic poet Percy Bysshe Shelley translated the *Homeric Hymn to Hermes* and made the story popular in the 19th century.

- Hermes features as the narrator in the musical *Hadestown*, where he describes himself as a man with feathers on his feet who can help you find your destination.

'Hermes, Messenger son of Zeus and Giver of Good Things,' said
Apollo, 'would you like to lie on a couch with golden Aphrodite,
even if tightly bound by strong chains?' Hermes the Messenger
and Slayer of Argus replied, 'Lord Apollo, you could bind me
three times as tight – or more – and invite all the gods and even
the goddesses to watch, if only I could lie with Aphrodite!'
When he said this, laughter arose among the immortal gods.

Odyssey 8.335ff.

☞ Fresco of Hermes from Pompeii,
1st century CE, National Archaeological
Museum, Naples

ARES

(ROMAN MARS)
'God of War'
The archetypal WARRIOR

ORIGIN STORY: Ares was the legitimate son of Zeus and Hera, and lover of Aphrodite. His full brother was Hephaestus and he had half-brothers and sisters in Hermes, Dionysus, Apollo, Artemis and Athena. His uncles were Poseidon and Hades, and he called Hestia 'aunt'.

JOB DESCRIPTION: ruthless soldier, hot-headed warrior, cold-hearted killer, terrorist, berserker, sometimes protector and butt of jokes. He is so archetypal that on vases he is often indistinguishable from anonymous soldiers preparing to leave home for battle – a popular subject. In many ways he is like Achilles, the key figure in Homer's *Iliad*. Both are swift, strong and ruthless. At one point the 'spirit of Ares' enters Achilles (*Iliad* 17.210).

GOD OF: warriors and soldiers and, in his Roman guise of Mars Silvanus, protector of boundaries between fields and woods.

> ### BATTLE TRAUMA
> A 1994 book by Jonathan Shay entitled *Achilles in Vietnam* compares the experiences of soldiers who fought in the Vietnam War (1955–73) with the warriors of the Trojan War. Shay found that the experiences of horror, terror, guilt and grief have not changed in three thousand years. In particular, he explores the concept of a warrior so overcome by rage that he goes 'berserk' and becomes an almost invincible killing machine. The first word of the *Iliad* is 'rage', *menis* in Greek.

SIGNIFICANT OTHERS: The god of war never married but did have affairs with many females, most famously Aphrodite. He wooed Persephone but did not win her. He has no male lovers until the 2nd-century Roman poet Lucian gives him Alectryon, who was later transformed into a cockerel.

APPEARANCE: Sometimes Ares is mature and bearded, other times he is young and clean-shaven. In Greek art, he is almost always shown wearing armour and brandishing a spear or sword and sometimes a shield. In his Roman guise as Mars, he is often naked apart from a golden helmet when with his wife Venus and assorted cupids.

EPITHETS: Man-murdering, Lover of War, Lover of Horses, Brutish, Bloodstained, Manslaughtering, Stormer of City Walls, Bane of Men, Fighter behind the Shield, Spear-carrying, Armed with Bronze, Bronze, Flesh-piercing and Sharp. (These last few are also used to describe spears.)

ANIMAL & PLANT ASSOCIATIONS: serpent, dragon, bear, vulture, woodpecker, wolf.

WHERE TO FIND HIM: In Athens, the Areopagus (literally 'Hill of Ares') is a rocky outcrop in the shadow of the Acropolis where Ares was supposedly tried for murdering a son of the sea god Poseidon. It became the place where murder trials were held and later a place where the Athenian council could meet to make decisions of state. Ares also has connections with Thrace (modern Bulgaria and southern Romania). In a tragedy of Euripides, Thracians are said to be 'a race inspired by Ares' (*Hecuba* 1090).

WHERE ON EARTH IS THRACE?

WHERE ON EARTH IS THRACE?

Thrace appears quite a lot in Greek myths but where on earth is it? I had no idea so, when I found out, I lit upon a fun visual mnemonic. Imagine the top view of a crab with its two pincers facing down. The pincer on the left is Greece and that on the right (a bit of) modern Turkey. Above these, the body of the crab is Thrace: modern Bulgaria and Romania. The Greeks always considered Thrace a bit of a savage backwater and source of strange customs and people. Poor Ovid was exiled to Thrace, by that time a Roman province.

The war god plays a more positive role in Roman mythology, where Ares counterpart, Mars, seduces a Vestal Virgin named Rhea Silvia who gives birth to Romulus and Remus, Rome's twin founders. This made him one of the ancestors of the Roman people, along with Venus via her son Aeneas. Mars also gave his name to March, the first month of the Roman year. He is suitably the patron god of conquering Rome.

SOME OF HIS BEST-KNOWN MYTHS:
As a powerful warrior, Ares epitomizes the Greek idea of masculinity. Because of this, it is a great achievement when others get the better of him, as when Hephaestus humiliates him by catching him with Aphrodite (see page 26). It is even worse when he is bested in battle. Athena helps the heroes Diomedes and Heracles to wound him at different times and he is also overcome by two giants named Ephialtes and Otus and imprisoned in a bronze jar for 13 months (*Iliad* 5.385). In ancient Greece, humiliation was the worst fate that could befall a Greek male, even worse than death.

Bronze statuette of Mars (Ares) from the Rhine, 3rd century CE, British Museum

THE SOFTER SIDE OF ARES:

The god of war gained some much-needed depth and humour in Roman time,s when he was often pictured as a boyishly handsome warrior dallying with Venus or being disarmed by mischievous cupids.

FUN FACTS ABOUT ARES:

- He has almost as many offspring as his father Zeus.
- The name Ares can be used as a metonymic stand-in for war.
- Ares features prominently in *Xena: Warrior Princess* and the Percy Jackson book series. He is also in Marvel's *The Mighty Avengers* and the later *Dark Avengers*, where he is given the character of a Hollywood drill sergeant like Sergeant Foley in *An Officer and a Gentleman* (1982) or Major Reisman in *The Dirty Dozen* (1967). The Marvel comics use Ares to explore what it is to be a soldier, whereas in the DC comic universe he is mostly the personification of war.

CLASSICAL ART TIME PERIODS

Art historians have divided Greek and Roman art into basic but helpful time chunks:

Protogeometric – before writing and before much decoration

Geometric – vases mostly decorated with circles and zigzags – 900–700 BCE

Archaic – influences from the Near East bring in stiff, smiling figures – 700–480 BCE*

Classical – the ideal body in relaxed poses; Athens at its zenith – 480–323 BCE**

Hellenistic – more drama and exaggeration – 323–30 BCE

Roman – imitation and adaptation of earlier Greek styles – 30 BCE – 400 CE

* 480 BCE saw the Battle of Salamis when the Greeks defeated the Persians at sea.

** 323 BCE was the year of Alexander the Great's death.

Come, warlike Mars! Put down your shield and
spear for a little while, and let your shining hair
free from its helmet. You might ask what business
a poet has with a warrior? Because you gave your
name to the month of which I now sing: March!

Ovid, Fasti 3.1ff.

Ares armed for war on a vase *c.*455 BCE, British Museum

APOLLO

(ROMAN APOLLO)
'God of Music, Prophecy and Healing'
The archetypal GOLDEN BOY

ORIGIN STORY: Apollo is the son of Zeus and Leto, one of the female Titans. When Leto conceived twins, jealous Hera found out and pursued her. Finally Leto found refuge on the floating island of Delos, also known as Ortygia (Quail Island). Clinging to a palm tree, she first gave birth to Artemis who immediately acted as midwife to help her twin brother Apollo into the world.

JOB DESCRIPTION: Also known as Phoebus ('Bright'), he is a pursuer of nymphs, provider of light and healing, punisher through disease and plague.

GOD OF: music, poetry, the sun, archery, reason, logic, musicians, poets, doctors and seers.

SIGNIFICANT OTHERS: Apollo loved all nine of the Muses. Unable to choose between them, he remained unmarried and enjoyed an active sex life with dozens of females and males, most notably Cyrene, Coronis, Daphne, Hecate, Adonis, Hyacinthus, Hymenaeus and Cyparissus. Apollo's son is Asclepius, god of healing.

APPEARANCE: With long wavy hair and a perfect physique, he is almost always shown as a beardless ephebe (youth) and is the epitome of beauty. Apollo is one of the few males who can pull off a man-bun. If he is in a peaceful mood, he will be holding his lyre. If he is in war mode, he wields bow and arrows, like his sister Artemis.

～

Said Apollo, 'The lyre and the curving bow will always be dear to me, and I will proclaim the infallible will of Zeus.'
Homeric Hymn to Delian Apollo
131ff.

～

61

EPITHETS: Apollo of the Silver Bow, Bow-carrying, Far-shooter, Phoebus of Uncut Hair, Golden-haired, Mouse Lord, Delphinius (God of Dolphins), God of Gnats, God of Locusts, Healer, Physician, Twin, Averter of Evil, Lizard Killer, Prophet, Leader of the Muses and so on.

ANIMAL & PLANT ASSOCIATIONS: mouse (linked to plague), raven (linked to prophecy), laurel (bay tree).

WHERE TO FIND HIM: Although he was born on the island of Delos in the Aegean Sea, his most impressive sanctuary is the dramatic mountaintop at Delphi on the Greek mainland, considered to be the navel of the world. The Delphic oracle, located beneath his temple there, was the most famous of all oracles. It is still a must-see destination in Greece. Apollo had many other oracles across the Mediterranean.

ONE OF HIS BEST-KNOWN MYTHS: An often told story is one about a woman named Niobe who boasted that she had far more offspring than Leto, who had only two. But Leto's two children were no ordinary children: they were Apollo and Artemis. When Leto heard of Niobe's boast, she sent Apollo to kill all Niobe's sons and Artemis to kill the daughters. Apollo killed six sons

according to the earliest source, and seven according to later sources, while Artemis polished off the daughters. Poor Niobe was eventually turned into a stone that you can still see on Mount Sipylus, near modern İzmir in Turkey. Apollo's arrows could bring death individually, as in the case of Niobe's sons, or in great number, as with the plague he brings at the beginning of the *Iliad*. But his arrows can also cure, and Apollo's son Asclepius is the god of healing and medicine.

THE SOFTER SIDE OF APOLLO: Apollo was charmed by music from the first moment he heard baby Hermes strum the newly invented lyre. The passion that music arouses in him is shown in a red-figure vase by the so-called Berlin Painter. The god's head is thrown back as he strums a lyre and his mouth is open as he sings his song.

〜

Leto's famous son comes to rocky Pytho, strumming his hollow lyre and wearing fragrant clothes…
Homeric Hymn to Pythian Apollo 182ff.

〜

62

GODS & THEIR PLANETS

Did the myths begin as stories to help people explain the pattern and movement of stars? Planets look like stars but they don't move in the same way; they seem to wander back and forth. (The Greek *planao* means 'I wander'.) Each planet is named after one of the Roman gods: Mercury, Venus, Mars, Jupiter, Neptune and Pluto, plus their ancestors Uranus and Saturn (Cronus). Creepily, some of Jupiter's moons are named after his conquests: Io, Europa, Callisto, Ganymede and so on. Apollo doesn't have a planet, probably because he is associated with the sun, just as his sister Artemis is linked to the moon. However, Apollo did give his name to the space programme that put the first human on the moon.

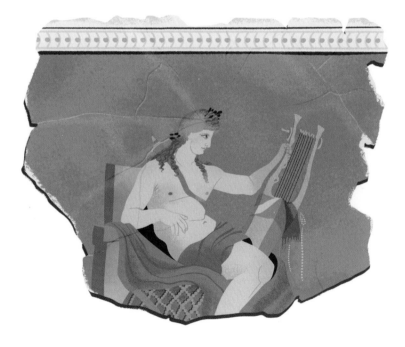

Fresco of Apollo with lyre, 1st century CE, Palatine Museum, Rome

FUN FACTS ABOUT APOLLO:

- Apollo is strongly associated with the mountain sanctuary Delphi, site of his famous oracle. The Pythia was a female seer who gave prophecies in a sacred space beneath his temple there. Her title honoured a monstrous snake named Pytho that Apollo slew at Delphi. And so he is often called Pythian Apollo.

- There are two Homeric Hymns to Apollo: one to Delian Apollo and one to Pythian Apollo.

- Some Greeks envisioned plagues and mass outbreaks of disease as a rain of arrows showering down on them from above. This is why Apollo and Artemis are associated with sickness, and yet also with being able to cure sickness.

- Like his father Zeus, Apollo often pursued and seduced nymphs. One nymph who was reluctant to be possessed by him was Daphne. She fled from his advances, but he was faster. As he got close, she begged Zeus to help her. Zeus changed her into a laurel tree and from then on Apollo always wore a laurel wreath.

- Bernini's breathtaking marble statue of Apollo grasping Daphne as she turns into a laurel tree was carved between 1622 and 1625. It can be found in the Borghese Gallery in Rome.

- Apollonian vs Dionysian: in the 1870s, the German philosopher Friedrich Nietzsche proposed Apollo as an archetype of calm restraint in contrast with Dionysus who would represent passionate abandon. Although it is true that Dionysus was god of the lack of inhibitions and mob mentality, he could also be calmly detached. And 'rational' Apollo often lost his temper. Near the beginning of Homer's *Iliad* (1.44–7), Apollo's fury sets in motion the death of Hector. Nietzsche believed early Athenian tragedy was the perfect synthesis of Apollonian and Dionysian (at least until the influence of the philosopher Socrates skewed it more towards the Apollonian).

- An episode of the classic TV series *Star Trek* from 1970 has Captain Kirk and his pals encounter a powerful being on an alien planet who claims to be Apollo and demands worship. The episode's title, 'Who Mourns for Adonais?', is taken from the poem 'Adonais: An Elegy on the Death of John Keats' by Percy Bysshe Shelley, based on an elegy by the 1st-century BCE Greek poet Bion.

Which of the gods made Achilles
and Agamemnon quarrel? It was the son
of Zeus and Leto [Apollo], for he was
angry with King Agamemnon.

Iliad 1.8

〜

Heracles tries to take the Delphic tripod from
Apollo on a vase *c.*475 BCE, British Museum

ARTEMIS

(ROMAN DIANA)
'Goddess of the Hunt'
The archetypal TOMBOY

ORIGIN STORY: Artemis is Apollo's twin sister, born of Zeus and Leto on the floating island of Delos, also known as Ortygia (Quail Island). She was born first and, being a goddess, was immediately able to become a midwife and help her mother deliver Apollo. For this reason, Artemis is one of the goddesses associated with childbirth.

JOB DESCRIPTION: huntress, eternal virgin, lover of girls, man hater, midwife, bringer of death by sickness.

GODDESS OF: the hunt, archery, woods, wild animals, childbirth, boundaries, girls who don't want to marry, hunters and women in childbirth.

SIGNIFICANT OTHERS: Virgin Artemis loved running wild with her entourage of maidens, many of whom she loved. Although she is much desired by men, she was one of the three goddesses immune to Aphrodite's power, according to Hesiod. She (possibly) loved only one male, the hunter Orion. But she never slept with him and always retained her virginity.

APPEARANCE: Artemis is usually shown wearing a diadem, sandals and a *chiton* (tunic) pulled up above her knees like an ancient miniskirt to give her freedom of movement. The so-called *Diana of Versailles* – a marble sculpture of the 2nd century BCE in the Louvre, based on an older Greek bronze original, shows her in this iconic dress with bow, arrow and a deer. She is deeply associated with deer, and although she hunts them, she also befriends them and occasionally rides them or gets them to pull her chariot.

AETIOLOGICAL STORIES

One of the jobs of myth was aetiological – that is, to explain the causes of things. The Greek word *aitia* means 'blame' as well as 'cause', and these origin stories often involve transformation with a sense of wrongdoing at the root, as if the change was a punishment of sorts.

Why does that constellation look like a bear? Why does the peacock seem to have 'eyes' on his tail? Why are spiders such good spinners? Many birds and a few trees were once virgins fleeing from would-be rapists, on whom a sympathetic god or goddess took pity. Some pools and springs came from weeping nymphs. Almost every flower, tree, bird and animal has a myth associated with it, and most involve the gods.

EPITHETS: Queen of Beasts, Daughter of Leto, Far-shooting, Of the Hunt, Arrow-Pourer, Delights in Arrows, Of the Golden Arrows, Of the Golden Throne, Of the Golden Reins, Strong-voiced, Chaste and dozens more, mostly to do with the many shrines associated with her.

ANIMAL & PLANT ASSOCIATIONS: hunting dog, deer, quail, palm tree.

WHERE TO FIND HER: The Temple of Artemis at Ephesus was one of the Seven Wonders of the World. Sadly, it no longer exists. The so-called Temple of Diana at Baiae near Naples is actually the remains of the dome of a grand bathhouse. Artemis/Diana was hugely popular, with varying attributes and abilities according to where she was worshipped; shrines and altars devoted to her can be found almost everywhere in the ancient world.

TWO OF HER BEST-KNOWN MYTHS: There are many versions of the myth of Actaeon and his hounds. Essentially, a young man named Actaeon is out hunting deer with his hounds when he accidentally comes upon Artemis bathing with her band of nymphs. He makes the fatal mistake of lingering to watch. Her vicious punishment is to make his own hounds tear him apart.

This story was told in a lost tragedy by Aeschylus and, five hundred years later, by the Roman poet Ovid, who has the hounds devour Actaeon because Diana (Artemis) has turned him into a deer. This was a popular myth on vases and signet rings. Sometimes Actaeon is in human form with a dog biting his leg; sometimes he is shown with antlers sprouting from his head as he turns to flee in terror from Diana's pointing finger.

In another story found in Ovid, Jupiter takes the form of Diana to seduce one of her entourage, an Arcadian princess named Callisto. One hot day the huntresses decide to bathe, and when Callisto is discovered to be pregnant, Diana furiously sends her away. Callisto gives birth to a healthy boy, Arcas, but jealous Juno finds out and changes her into a bear. Flash-forward 15 years to Arcas hunting in the woods. Suddenly a she-bear approaches him, arms extended to embrace him. Terrified, Arcas is about to kill his bear-mother when Jupiter intervenes and sweeps them both up to the heavens to become the constellations Ursa Major and Ursa Minor, the Big Bear and the Little Bear.

☞ Terracotta figurine of Artemis on a throne c. 350 BCE, British Museum

≈

I sing of Artemis, of the Golden Arrows, calling out to her hounds – the eternal maiden – running over shadowed mountains to shoot stags…She rejoices in archery and draws the bow, exulting in the chase.
Homeric Hymn to Artemis 1ff.

≈

THE SOFTER SIDE OF ARTEMIS:

Although she can be the ultimate mean girl, with the cold cruelty of many adolescents, Artemis is just a girl. Her arrows stand for death by sickness rather than violence. Andromache, wife of Hector, tells how, after the violent deaths of her father and brothers, Artemis the 'arrow-pourer' slew her mother, as if it were a mercy (*Iliad* 6.425ff.). Penelope, the long-suffering wife of Odysseus, also prays for the 'arrows of Artemis'. It seems that Artemis occupied herself with girls and women, and her brother Apollo took boys and men. Because Artemis and her brother were associated with the arrow-strike of sudden sickness, they could also heal.

FUN FACTS ABOUT ARTEMIS:

- There is a version of Artemis so unlike her classical Greek incarnation that it is arguable whether she is the same deity. In statues of this Near Eastern version, often known as the Lady of Ephesus, she is covered with breasts or possibly testicles.
- According to some ancient writers, Artemis allowed one boy to join her entourage of virgins. His name was Daphnis, son of Hermes, and he was a musician.
- In the *Aeneid*, the poet Virgil invents a princess named Camilla who has been dedicated to Diana by her father, who raises her in the woods. He feeds her mare's milk when she is a baby, dresses her in animal skins and teaches her to hunt as soon as she can walk. When older, she dresses as an Amazon to fight the invading Trojans and is eventually killed by one of Aeneas' allies.
- Artemis is the polar opposite of her brother Apollo. He embodies civilization; she loves to run wild. He is sexually active; she is a virgin. Apollo rules the day and, in later times, was associated with the sun, whereas Artemis loves hunting at night and was eventually linked to the moon.

Odysseus' wife Penelope:
'If only virgin Artemis would bring me
soft death, right now, so that I should
not waste my life in mourning…'
Odyssey 18.202ff.

Artemis rides a deer and a satyr follows on a vase *c.*355 BCE, British Museum

DEMETER

(ROMAN CERES)
'Goddess of Grain'
The archetypal HELICOPTER MOTHER

ORIGIN STORY: Demeter is one of the six children of Rhea and Cronus, sister to Zeus, Hera and the others. Whereas her divine sister Hestia is a sedentary virgin, fertile Demeter is a roaming goddess, causing the earth to produce abundantly.

JOB DESCRIPTION: producer of crops, mother of Persephone, bereaved mother, controller of the cycle of life, key goddess in an important mystery cult.

GODDESS OF: grain, dealers in grain, farmers, fertility, death and rebirth, and those who undergo initiation in the Eleusinian Mysteries.

SIGNIFICANT OTHERS: Demeter is not officially married but being a goddess of fruitfulness she has many lovers. With her brother Zeus she has a daughter, Persephone. With another brother, Poseidon, she also gave birth to Areion (a horse) and Despoine (a goddess). She also loved Iasion, Carmanor and Mecon.

APPEARANCE: In Greek art, Demeter is often shown with her mantle covering her head (although not her face) in an attitude of modesty and also bereavement. She mostly accessorizes with wheat, but can also be spotted with torch, sceptre, bread, wine jug and/or a cup of *kykeon*, her special drink.

EPITHETS: Bringer of Divine Order, With Long Yellow Hair, Dark-robed, Honoured, Furious, The Dark and so on.

WHERE TO FIND HER: Eleusis, near Athens, where she finally collapsed after searching long and hard for her beloved daughter Persephone, who had been abducted by Hades. She is deeply connected with the Eleusinian Mysteries.

THE ELEUSINIAN MYSTERIES

A 'mystery' religion is any cult that by secret teaching and/or mysterious rituals could show people the best ways of existing after death, whether by pointing the soul to the best part of the underworld, showing it how to navigate the heavens, or even ensuring it could choose the best new body in which to be reborn. Undergoing an initiation also created a more personal bond with the god, and increased the chances of your offerings being accepted.

There were several mystery cults in the Graeco-Roman world. Unfortunately, because the teaching and rituals were top secret, we know very little for certain about what went on. The Eleusinian Mysteries were the most famous of several mystery cults, possibly because Eleusis (the place where Demeter stopped in her search for Persephone and the focus of the cult) was local to Athens. Among other things, the Eleusinian Mysteries may have involved a night-time re-enactment of the story of Demeter and Persephone.

ONE OF HER BEST-KNOWN MYTHS:

When her young daughter Persephone is abducted by Hades, god of the underworld, Demeter neglects her job of making crops grow to search for her. She wanders the land in disguise and finally collapses at Eleusis, a town about 6 miles (10 km) north-west of Athens. She is shown hospitality by the family of the town's king, Celeus, but continues to grieve for many days, neither smiling nor speaking, neither eating nor drinking until the servant Iambe makes her laugh and cheers her up. Celeus' wife, Metaneira, fortifies Demeter with a non-alcoholic drink made of water, grain and mint (or possibly pennyroyal). This strange version of barley water became the basis for *kykeon*, the mysterious drink that was a vital part of the Eleusinian mysteries.

To thank the family for reviving her, Demeter becomes nursemaid to their little boys, Demophon and Triptolemus. The milk from her breast is so powerful that Triptolemus grows at an extraordinary rate. She bathes Demophon in ambrosia and roasts him in sacred fire to burn away his mortality. Coming upon this ritual one day, their mother screams. Angry at the interruption, Demeter declares that she will not make the boy immortal after all. She reveals herself to be a goddess and instructs the Eleusinians to build her a temple and an altar. 'I will instruct you in the rites myself,' she tells them, 'so that you can faithfully observe them and win back my favour' (*Homeric Hymn to Demeter* 273ff.). This whole business is a strange interruption in Demeter's quest for Persephone but explains the very ancient rites at Eleusis, which presumably allowed participants to obtain some part of the immortality denied the boy in the fire.

Resuming her search for Persephone, Demeter withholds all the crops from the world until Zeus commands that her daughter be returned to her. Hades reluctantly agrees, but tricks Persephone into eating a pomegranate seed. This ties her to the underworld for eternity and she must spend part of every year there, the season when Demeter does not produce crops but mourns her daughter's absence.

KYKEON

The mysterious drink that first revived Demeter and later was used in the Eleusinian Mysteries is much discussed. In the *Iliad*, *kykeon* is a mixture of wine and barley with goats' cheese grated on top. In the *Odyssey*, the sorceress Circe makes it with honey and a mystery ingredient. Some scholars think a type of grain fungus called ergot might have given the drink hallucinogenic properties. Traces of this fungus have been found at another site where the Eleusinian Mysteries were celebrated.

THE HARSHER SIDE OF DEMETER:

Although we might expect the goddess of grain to be nurturing and bountiful, Demeter can be shockingly cruel. Perhaps we can put some of this down to the grief she feels at the loss of her daughter. Once, while searching for Persephone, she came to a house and asked for refreshment. The woman of the house offered her a form of *kykeon* and Demeter gulped it so hastily that the son mocked her. In revenge, she flung the rest of the drink at him and he became a gecko. From that day on she always blessed anyone who killed a gecko. She also became angry at a nymph named Minthe, who had been the lover of Hades before he desired Persephone. When Minthe boasted that she was better and more beautiful than Persephone, Demeter furiously stamped her into the ground where she became a fragrant herb: mint.

FUN FACTS ABOUT DEMETER:

- She never married but had several lovers, one of whom may have been Dionysus in his guise as Iacchus.
- Triptolemus, one of the babies she nursed while searching for Persephone, became a very important figure. Demeter taught him the art of agriculture and he travelled around Greece in a flying chariot, teaching everyone how to plant crops. He is a popular character on Greek vases and seems to have played an important part in the Eleusinian Mysteries.
- According to Hesiod, Demeter loved a hero named Iasion and gave birth to Ploutus (the god of wealth), who is different from Pluto (Hades) but often confused or conflated with him.
- In the *Lore Olympus* webcomic, Demeter is CEO of a company called Barley Mother.

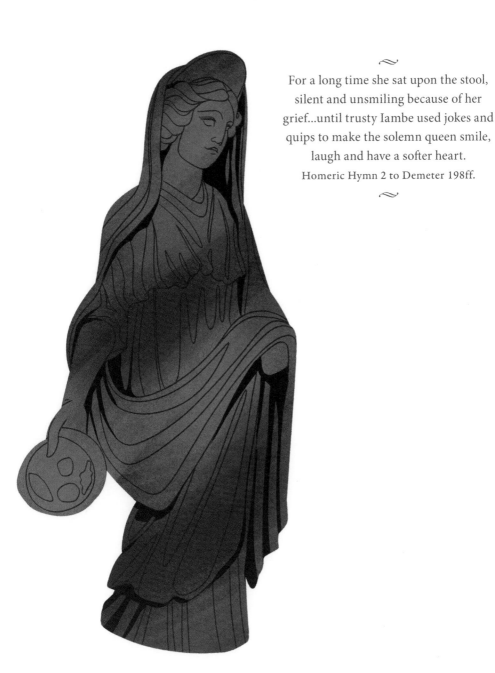

For a long time she sat upon the stool,
silent and unsmiling because of her
grief...until trusty Iambe used jokes and
quips to make the solemn queen smile,
laugh and have a softer heart.

Homeric Hymn 2 to Demeter 198ff.

Bronze figurine of Ceres (Demeter), 1st century CE, British Museum

HESTIA

(ROMAN VESTA)
'Goddess of the Hearth'
The archetypal SAFE HAVEN

ORIGIN STORY: One of the three daughters of Cronus, her sisters are Hera and Demeter. As the first-born child of Cronus and Rhea (according to most accounts), she was the first one swallowed and therefore the last disgorged. So she is both eldest and youngest of the Olympians. Wooed by Poseidon and Apollo, she asked her brother Zeus if she could remain a virgin for ever and he agreed. Therefore she has no children.

JOB DESCRIPTION: She tends the hearth, the central flame in a home used for lighting, warmth, cooking and protection. She sets an example to the Greek wife on how to be nurturing, welcoming and warm.

GODDESS OF: the hearth, fire, loaves of bread, stories, thresholds, shelter and anyone who likes warmth, light and a hot meal, from kings to enslaved persons.

SIGNIFICANT OTHERS: Hestia is one of the three goddesses immune to Aphrodite's power and therefore has no lovers or spouse. However, in one of the Homeric Hymns the poet shows Hestia and Hermes together as friends.

APPEARANCE: We rarely see Hestia, but when we do she is dressed in long robes, often with her head covered for extra modesty. She can accessorize with a sceptre or a flowering branch. Hestia and Demeter have many similarities. On coins both are shown with covered heads and they walk next to each other towards the wedding of Peleus and Thetis on a black-figured bowl called the Sophilos Dinos in the British Museum. A Pompeian fresco believed to be of Hestia in her guise as

THE PALLADIUM

The Palladium was an ancient and mysterious effigy of Athena that played an important part in the Trojan War and in the foundation of Rome. Made of wood and small enough to be carried, it had great power to protect the city in which it resided. Retellings of a story in the lost *Little Iliad* relate how Odysseus and/or Diomedes infiltrated Troy to steal the Palladium. After the destruction of Troy, it stayed with Diomedes for a while. Virgil has Aeneas bring it from Troy to his new homeland in Italy, where it was eventually housed in the Temple of Vesta in Rome. This is how an ancient artefact from long vanished Troy ended up under the protection of Rome's version of Hestia, goddess of the hearth.

᙮

Nor does Hestia love the deeds
of Aphrodite. That modest girl
was the first born child of crafty
Cronus and the youngest, too.
Homeric Hymn to Aphrodite 21ff.

᙮

Vesta shows her holding a cornucopia and pouring a libation onto a fire, while a donkey stands behind her. This fresco is from the shrine in a bakery, where donkeys pulled millstones to grind grain. But the donkey also reminds us of the time this animal preserved her chastity (see opposite).

EPITHETS: Respected Virgin, Mistress (*potnia*), Queen (*basileia*), Golden-Throned and so on.

ANIMAL & PLANT ASSOCIATIONS: pig, swine, donkey, the chaste tree (*Vitex agnus-castus*).

WHERE TO FIND HER: The Greek goddess Hestia had very few free-standing temples dedicated to her as she was worshipped at the altars of all the temples of all the gods. The famous Temple of Vesta in Rome was where the city's sacred fire was kept burning at all times, tended by the six Vestal Virgins. This temple did not contain a cult image of Vesta (the flame represented her) but it did house the Palladium, a small effigy of Minerva said to have been brought from Troy by Aeneas. You can see the partly reconstructed remains of the Temple of Vesta in the Roman Forum. It is a charming round building with three columns still standing.

ONE OF HER BEST-KNOWN MYTHS:
The Roman poet Ovid tells how once, at a banquet of the gods, randy Priapus spotted sleeping Vesta/Hestia. He was about to have his wicked way with her when a donkey brayed a warning. The gods quickly rescued her and thrashed Priapus. This may be why a donkey sometimes features in depictions of Vesta.

~

Stay in this glorious house
in friendship together, Hestia
and Hermes…
Homeric Hymn to Hestia 21ff.

~

Hestia with flowers on a vase, 5th century BCE, National Archaeological Museum, Tarquinia

THE SOFTER SIDE OF HESTIA: Hestia has become my favourite member of the Pantheon. She is goddess of the hearth with its flame that supplies warmth, light, cooked food and stories (best told around a fire) – in short, everything you could want in life. Hestia is calm and nurturing. She does not fight with the other gods or take sides. She does not torture or punish people for their hubris. She has no lovers and she is not married. She stays at home by the hearth and in a way she *is* the hearth. She is so dependable and loving that you almost take her for granted. When Alcestis is dying in the famous play by Euripides, she prays at Hestia's hearth-altar, asking the goddess to look after her children (*Alcestis* 162ff.).

~

Father Zeus gave Hestia the
good gift of honour instead of
marriage. She got the richest
portion and seated herself in the
middle of the house.
Homeric Hymn to Aphrodite 29ff.

~

Bdelycleon: What's that thing?
Philocleon: The pigpen for the swine
to be sacrificed to Hestia.
Bdelycleon: Did you steal it from
her shrine?
Aristophanes, Wasps 845ff.

☞ Hestia (?) from the Parthenon,
438–432 BCE, British Museum

WHAT IS A CORNUCOPIA?

A cornucopia is literally a 'horn of abundance'. It is sometimes also called a 'horn of plenty'. The things in the cornucopia are invariably good: fruit, grain, loaves and so on.

Why are the good things in a horn-shaped container? Possibly because ancient harvesters slung cone-shaped baskets over their shoulders for collecting produce. However, the mythical explanation is that when baby Zeus was growing up hidden in a cave, one of his attendants was a goat called Amaltheia who suckled him. One day baby Zeus accidentally broke off one of her horns. From then on, this horn had the power to provide for all his needs in abundance.

Gods shown accessorizing with a cornucopia include Zeus, Dionysus, Fortuna (the personification of good luck) and especially Hades and his alter-ego Ploutus (the god of wealth). Cornucopia is a Latin word. The Greek word for cornucopia is *keras* ('horn') and was also used to describe a horn-shaped drinking vessel. In some cases it is not clear whether Hades is holding a giant drinking vessel or an empty cornucopia. Either way, it stands for bounty.

FUN FACTS ABOUT HESTIA:

- 'Hestia comes first' was a saying among the Greeks and the Romans because not only was she the first-born child of Cronus and Rhea but offerings were made to her first.
- She did not fight in the Gigantomachy (the battle of gods and giants, see page 103) because she remained on Olympus, literally keeping the home fires burning.
- Hestia is sometimes linked to Hephaestus because both rule the realm of fire.
- Sedentary Hestia is often teamed with Hermes as both bless thresholds and borders.
- Each Greek city had its own sacred fire of Hestia, and if some of the citizens left to establish a new colony, they would take some of her sacred fire with them.
- Swan Vesta matches are partly named after the goddess, and in the Victorian period 'vesta' became a synonym for match.
- Hestia makes a brief appearance in the TV series *Xena: Warrior Princess*, in the episode 'Warrior...Priestess...Tramp' (S3E9). Her priestess, Leah, a comically virgin lookalike of Xena, appears in this and several other episodes. In the *Star Wars* TV series *The Mandalorian*, the female Armorer is a combination of Hestia and Hephaestus.

~

Zeus, the great leader in the heavens, goes first.
He drives a winged chariot, having arranged and
ordered all things. An army of gods and divinities
follows behind. They are drawn up in eleven
squadrons, for Hestia alone remains in the
house of the gods.

Plato, Phaedrus 246eff.

~

83

DIONYSUS

(ROMAN BACCHUS, IACCHUS & LIBER PATER)
'God of Wine and Drama'
The archetypal RAVE LEADER

ORIGIN STORY: Zeus seduced Semele, a beautiful Theban princess. Jealous Hera found out and convinced Semele to ask Zeus to appear to her in his true nature, knowing that no mortal could survive exposure to an Olympian in their pure glory. When Zeus displayed his true nature, poor Semele burst into flames. Zeus snatched the baby from her womb and sewed it into his thigh. In due time, Dionysus ('twice born') came into the world.

JOB DESCRIPTION: Dionysus is the god of release, of the sense of the loss of self in communal experiences such as music, dance and drama, as well as the sharing of wine. Although Dionysus was into altered mental states, cross-dressing and raves, he was also the god of storytelling and a psychopomp (he led souls down to Hades). he was a god of fertility. The god of wine also loved a boy named Ampelos, whose name means 'grapevine'. Like modern cult leaders, Dionysus could become abusive. The 2nd-century CE Roman author Nonnus has him drug the nymph Nicaea and wind goddess Aura with wine before assaulting them.

GOD OF: wine, ecstasy, altered states, actors, playwrights, vintners and all manufacturers of grape-related products.

SIGNIFICANT OTHERS: Dionysus loved Ariadne, Althaea, Erigone, Nicaea, Pallene and the goddess Aphrodite who gave birth to their son Priapus, always shown in a state of arousal to indicate

Dionysus:
I put on a
fawn-skin and took up my
thyrsus, my ivy javelin.
Euripides, The Bacchae 24ff.

APPEARANCE: Sometimes Dionysus is depicted as youthfully clean-shaven and sometimes as a robed man with long hair and beard. He either reclines with a *kantharos* (cup) of wine, or moves in some sort of procession with his entourage. Dionysus accessorizes with a thyrsus (see page 88), grapes and garland of vine leaves, plus maenads (uninhibited women) and satyrs (lusty goat-men). He is often accompanied by his pet panther or leopard, a reminder that in some versions of his story he journeys to India and back. A shrine-fresco from Pompeii shows the clean-shaven Dionysus as his Roman alter ego, Bacchus. He stands in front of lush pre-eruption Vesuvius wearing a massive cluster of deep-red grapes. He pours out a libation of wine and his pet leopard sneaks a taste.

EPITHETS: Twice-born, Thigh-born, Of the Trees, God of the Wine Press, Blossom Bringer, Branch Bearer, Ivy Bearer, Of the Vine Branch, Of the Fig Tree, Beer Lover, Bull-eating, Hidden, Of the Mysteries, Loosener, Androgynous, False Man, Ruler, Fox-skin-wearing, Of the Underworld, Bacchus the Comforter of Humankind... When involved in the Eleusinian Mysteries, he sometimes goes by the name Iacchus. When involved with viticulture he is known as Liber Pater (Free Father).

ANIMAL & PLANT ASSOCIATIONS: grapes and vines, ivy, fennel, artichoke, leopard, panther, lion, bull, dolphin, snakes.

WHERE TO FIND HIM: Dionysus has very few temples because he is mainly worshipped in the woods or in the theatre. However, he has a small temple on the south slope of the Acropolis in Athens, next to his most famous theatre. It was here that dozens of musical masked tragedies and comedies were performed during his festival, dramas that are now considered masterpieces of Western culture. Roman Bacchus has more temples than Dionysus, including one of the biggest in the world at Baalbek in Lebanon.

~

I will tell of Dionysus, son of glorious Semele, how he appeared on the shore of the barren sea, on a jutting promontory. He looked like a young man in the prime of youth: his beautiful dark hair floated about him and he had a purple cloak around his muscular shoulders.

Homeric Hymn to Dionysus 1ff.

~

Golden-haired Dionysus made
tawny Ariadne, daughter of Minos,
his shapely wife.
Hesiod, Theogony 947ff.

~

ONE OF HIS BEST-KNOWN MYTHS:

In one of the most shocking Athenian
tragedies to come down to us – *The
Bacchae* – Euripides tells how Dionysus
punished the Thebans for causing
his mother's death and refusing to
acknowledge him as a god. First, Dionysus
drives the women of Thebes mad and
forces them to worship him in a kind
of rave on the wooded slopes of Mount
Cithaeron. These 'maenads' include his
aunt Agave who was partly responsible
for his mother's death. Next, he convinces
Agave's son, the young king Pentheus,
to dress like a girl in order to spy on the
women and see what they are getting up
to. Dressed in female attire, Pentheus
climbs a pine tree. But the maenads,
possessed by ecstatic madness, spot him
and uproot the pine. Queen Agave thinks
her son is a lion cub, and she and the
maenads tear him limb from limb. She
proudly brings home his head impaled on a
thyrsus until, in a scene of horrific tragedy,
she gradually realizes what she is holding.

WHAT IS A MAENAD?

Maenads (pronounced MEE-nads) were
followers of Dionysus – usually city-dwell-
ing women who let their hair down when
they followed the god of wine into the
mountains and woods. There they entered
a state of ecstatic frenzy and became 'mad'.
(The verb *mainomai* means 'to become
mad' in both senses of anger and frenzy.)
In this altered state, brought on by dancing, music, wine, psychotropic drugs and
the power of the god, they could tear apart
forest creatures and uproot pine trees.
According to Euripides, they wore deer-
skin bodices and some of them suckled
fawns and wolf cubs. Maenads are hugely
popular subjects on Greek vases, often
shown following Dionysus or fleeing amorous satyrs.

~

Dionysus:
I, Dionysus, have come to
the land of the Thebans. I am
the son of Zeus by Semele,
prematurely born when he blasted
her with his glory.
Euripides, The Bacchae 1

~

WHAT IS A THYRSUS?

A thyrsus was a strange kind of staff or large wand carried by Dionysus and especially by his followers, the maenads. It was either a stalk of giant fennel wound about with ivy leaves and topped with a clump of ivy or a pinecone, or it was an artichoke on its tall stalk entwined with ivy. (Scholars cannot agree.) We see from vases that the thyrsus can be as tall as those who hold it. From Euripides' play *The Bacchae* we know the maenads twirled them as a sign to start the 'rave', raised them above their heads as they danced and used them as clubs or spears to attack animals and people. The thyrsus can be magical, too: one maenad strikes hers against a rock to bring forth water. They can also produce wine or honey. As Hugh Bowden said in a talk he gave for King's College London, 'When you think about festivals in the ancient world, don't think about the Parthenon, gods or statues. Think about Glastonbury.'

~

Dionysus to Pentheus:
You do not know why you live,
or what you are doing, or
who you are.
The Bacchae 506

~

THE SOFTER SIDE OF DIONYSUS: The ancient *Homeric Hymn to Dionysus* tells how the god calmly allowed himself to be kidnapped by pirates. Once out at sea, he caused the rigging to become grapevines and he took on the form of a lion. When the sailors jumped overboard in terror, he took pity on them and turned them into dolphins. Then he stretched out full length with his cornucopia (horn of good things, see page 82). This story is depicted on one of the great masterpieces of Greek art, a black-figure drinking cup by Exekias, one of the earliest great artists for whom we have a name.

Dionysus destroys a fawn on a vase,
5th century BCE, British Museum

FUN FACTS ABOUT DIONYSUS:

- The oldest image of him is on a wine-mixing bowl called the Sophilos Dinos in the British Museum in London, dated to about 575 BCE.
- Just as Apollo once dandled baby Hermes, so grown-up Hermes is often shown dandling his baby half-brother Dionysus.
- Euripides' play *The Bacchae* was the Roman emperor Nero's favourite Greek tragedy.
- Dionysus is one of the most androgynous of the gods, sometimes dressing as a girl or convincing others, like Pentheus, to do so. In one variant of his origin story, he was brought up as a girl in order to thwart attempts by Hera to kill him.
- On Athenian vases Dionysus is often surrounded by priapic satyrs and raving girls but he himself is almost always shown serenely in control. Even when he rips a fawn in half on a vase painted around 470 BCE he appears calm.
- Greek Dionysus and Roman Bacchus seem like two entirely different characters. Dionysus is young, slim and beautiful. Bacchus can be a chubby old buffoon with rolls of fat and a red nose. It is as if Dionysus had become his rustic old foster father Silenus.
- Dionysus appears in Disney's cartoon *Fantasia* (1940) as overweight and tipsy, riding a tiny unicorn donkey and lustily pursuing female centaurs to the tune of Ludwig van Beethoven's Symphony No. 6 'Pastoral'.

~

Pentheus to Dionysus:
You seem like a bull as you lead me out, with those horns growing from your head. You have become savage as a bull now.
The Bacchae 920

~

HADES

(ROMAN PLUTO)
'God of the Underworld'
The archetypal RICH BUT LONELY BOSS

ORIGIN STORY: One of the three sons of Cronus and Rhea, he was devoured, then freed, then assigned to be king of the underworld after choosing lots. His name means 'hidden', and it is also the name by which his realm – the underworld – is called.

JOB DESCRIPTION: When mortals die they must descend to the land of the dead and be judged. Hades (or one of his subordinates) sends them to various sections of the underworld, depending on their deeds.

GOD OF: death, judgement, the riches of the earth, dead souls.

SIGNIFICANT OTHERS: Persephone is his beloved wife while Minthe is an earlier old flame.

APPEARANCE: Like his brothers, Zeus and Poseidon, he is powerfully built and bearded. On Greek vases he is usually shown with dark hair but it can also be grey or white. He accessorizes with a staff, a cornucopia (to symbolize the mineral and agricultural riches of the earth) and his three-headed guard dog Cerberus.

EPITHETS: Because the Greeks feared to pronounce the name Hades, they used many alternate names such as Lord of Many, Lord of the Underworld, Dis, Ploutus and even The One with Many Names. Aidoneus is another of his names; it means 'unseen' and is very close to the god's actual name. The author of the Homeric Hymns calls him 'hateful' (*Homeric Hymn to Demeter* 395), and Homer calls him 'mighty' (*Iliad* 5.395).

ANIMAL & PLANT ASSOCIATIONS: cypress trees, narcissus flower, black sheep, multi-headed dogs.

WHERE TO FIND HIM: Because he is god of the dead, he does not have many temples in his honour, though he did have one in Elis, near Olympia, and an oracle by the river Acheron. His Roman counterpart, Pluto, had a temple in Dougga, Tunisia.

ONE OF HIS LEAST-KNOWN MYTHS: The Abduction of Persephone (see page 114) is without doubt the most famous story told about Hades. But several sources mention an obscure battle between him and Heracles that has not survived in full. Our earliest reference to this is from the *Iliad*, when Aphrodite is wounded by one of the Greek warriors in Book 5 and goes running to her mother, Dione, who comforts her daughter by reminding her of the time another mortal wounded not only Hera but also Hades. 'Mighty Hades suffered a sharp wound too,' says Dione, 'when Heracles the son of aegis-bearing Zeus bent his bow in Pylos among the corpses and caused him acute pain, piercing his muscular shoulder with an agonising arrow, so that his heart was sick and his spirit crushed...' (*Iliad* 5.395ff.).

There were several places called Pylos in Greece, and even the ancient commentators were not sure which one was meant. One Pylos, on the road between Olympia and Elis, was sacred to Hades, so perhaps this was the site of the mysterious battle between Heracles and Hades.

THE SOFTER SIDE OF HADES: His abduction of Persephone aside, Hades is not as cruel as some of the other gods. On rare occasions he is even inclined to show mercy. He lets Orpheus have a go at rescuing Eurydice (see page 116). And when Heracles comes to borrow the watchdog Cerberus in order to complete his twelfth and final task, Hades agrees. Although he rules the land of the dead, Hades is not evil but quite rational, even businesslike.

Despite a bad beginning, he and his wife Persephone have one of the most stable marriages among the Olympians. Like Hestia, he does not take sides in the Trojan War or in the affairs of mortals. A classicist friend of mine imagines him as an administrator, recording the ever-growing population of the dead, keeping accounts and making judgements all day long.

FUN FACTS ABOUT HADES:

- Apollo's son Asclepius was a superb physician who saved many sick people from death and occasionally revived some who had just died. This annoyed Hades, so he asked his brother Zeus to smite Asclepius with a thunderbolt. Zeus obliged, although later the dead Asclepius was deified and became the god of medicine.

- Hades (whose name can mean 'unseen') has a cap of invisibility, also known as the Helmet of Hades. It was made for him by a Cyclops (see page 184) after Hades, Zeus and Poseidon freed him from Tartarus. Perseus famously borrowed it (along with other gadgets from the gods) in order to slay Medusa.

- The most solemn oath a god can take is by the Styx, the river that separates the land of the living from the land of the dead.

- Pomegranates are a symbol of love, death and later of resurrection. And, according to some, if you cut a pomegranate in half, you will find a map of the underworld.

- In the musical *Hadestown* by Anaïs Mitchell, Hades is a major character, appearing in a pinstripe suit like a Mafia don.

- In the webcomic *Lore Olympus* the main story is the love affair between Persephone and Hades, who is portrayed as an emotionally wounded but considerate and desirable lover.

Youthful Hades (as Pluto) on a vase, 4th century BCE, British Museum

THE GEOGRAPHY OF THE UNDERWORLD

After death a person's immortal soul must go somewhere, usually underground. Living heroes and immortal gods must enter at various access points – Lake Avernus, for example – but the dead are immediately transported to the banks of the river Styx. In order to cross over and continue their journey, the soul must pay Charon the ferryman a small coin called an obol, which was why a coin was placed in the mouth of the dead. (Because they had no pockets, ancient Greeks sometimes carried small coins in their mouths.)

The bank of the river Styx is crowded with unburied souls yearning to continue their journey; these souls are often the ones that haunt the living. The lucky souls who reach the other side now pass by Cerberus, the three-headed hound. This threshold guardian is happy to let souls through the narrow gate, but less inclined to let them out.

Next, they come to the Fields of Asphodel where souls wander among weedlike flowers, squeaking sadly. In some accounts the souls must pass two pools, one of Lethe, of forgetfulness, and one of Mnemosyne, of remembering. (Those who have undergone initiation into the mysteries know to drink from the pool of remembering.)

Finally, the souls arrive at the palace of Hades and Persephone. Here in the forecourt sit three judges: Minos, Rhadamanthys and Aeacus. If the soul of the dead is judged to be very noble, the soul is sent to Elysium, the least unpleasant part of the underworld. Average souls go back to the Asphodel Fields and wicked souls to Tartarus, the darkest, bleakest place.

∾

Helios, the sun god, speaking to Demeter:
'Among the gods, Aidoneus King of Multitudes is not
an unsuitable son-in-law for your daughter.
The Lord of the Dead comes from your own line;
he is your brother. He was honoured with a share
equal to Zeus and Poseidon and he is king of those
who were allotted to him.'
Homeric Hymn to Demeter 84ff.

∾

Down in the underworld, Hades the lord of ghosts was gripped with fear. He jumped up from his throne and cried out, fearing that Earth-shaker Poseidon would split the earth above and expose his dark and dreadful home for all to see, both mortals and immortals.

Iliad 20.61ff.

☞ Hades as Persephone's husband on a vase *c.*340 BCE, British Museum

PRIMAL
DEITIES

The Olympians were actually third-generation gods. Before them came stranger, less human-looking gods, often called *protogenoi* – 'born first' or 'primordial'. These gods are not canonical like the deities of later monotheistic faiths, but rather they shift and change. The Greek farmer poet Hesiod, writing around the year 700 BCE, is our oldest and main source. He is not always clear or consistent because he is drawing upon much earlier oral sources, now lost. His work is a fascinating glimpse into ancient ideas of creation.

☞ Gaia hands Erechtheus to Athena on a drinking cup *c.*440 BCE, Berlin

CHAOS

'Chaos came first,' says Hesiod (*Theogony* 116). This is the first recorded use of the Greek word *chaos*. We don't really know what it means, so we simply transliterate the Greek. The word is related to the Greek verb meaning 'to gape' or 'to be open', and to the noun meaning 'chasm'. For Hesiod, Chaos is a giant yawn, a dark chasm full of emptiness. It's nothing, whereas for the Latin poet Ovid, writing seven hundred years after Hesiod, Chaos is a seething mass of all the elements combined. In the Hebrew Bible, parts of which were written around the same time as the *Theogony*, creation begins in a not dissimilar way: 'In the beginning, God created the heavens and the earth. And the earth was formless and void, and darkness was over the deep' (Genesis 1.1–2).

GAIA (Roman TERRA MATER)

'Next came broad-bosomed Gaia (Earth), a firm foundation for the immortal ones who live on the peaks of Olympus,' continues Hesiod (*Theogony* 117). Whereas Chaos was only there at the beginning, Gaia is hugely important and will endure throughout the generations of gods and humans. *Chaos* is a neuter word in Greek, but *Gaia* is Feminine with a capital F for fruitful, fertile and fecund. She is always pregnant or giving birth. Gaia will soon bring forth humans and animals, trees and plants, hills and seas. She will also bring forth monsters. She will even bring forth her consort and equal, Uranus, and from the two of them will come most of the gods and goddesses. Gaia is maternal and protects her offspring, and because of this she can be vindictive. This characteristic will show up in some of her descendants – Hera and Demeter, for example.

TARTARUS

Next to come into being is gloomy Tartarus, *Tartaros* in Greek – another neuter word – meaning 'dark abyss'. This is a terrible place. It will end up being the lowest part of the underworld and a prison for monsters to come. Only once is Tartarus personified, to mate with Gaia and bring forth Typhoeus (Roman Typhon), a strange volcanic storm giant with serpent's legs. He will father other monsters before Zeus imprisons him – confusingly – in his father, Tartarus.

EROS (Roman CUPID)

Aphrodite is the oldest of the Olympian gods, born from the severed genitals of Zeus' grandfather, Uranus, but somehow her 'son' Eros is even older. He is the last of the four 'first' things mentioned by Hesiod. Eros is already the personification of love in the sexual sense. (We get the word 'erotic' from Eros.) He is described as 'the most beautiful of the undying gods, the relaxer of limbs and seducer of the hearts and minds of all gods and men' (*Theogony* 120ff.). A few lines on in the *Theogony*, he will attend Aphrodite's birth. While the poet Sappho, writing a century after Hesiod, seems to give him Gaia and Uranus as parents, the poet Simonides, writing a half century later still, makes him the child of Aphrodite and Ares. Depicted in art as an adolescent boy, Eros often has wings, perhaps because love is fleeting.

Eros arouses love by violence; in his earliest depictions he is shown with a whip, an ox-goad or bow and arrows, as if the Greeks could not settle on what the beginning of love felt like. Sappho writes of being shaken by Eros rather than pierced. The famous desire-arousing arrows are not established until the late 5th century. Eros becomes Cupid in Roman times, and the poet Ovid gives him blunt, lead-tipped arrows to cause revulsion and sharp, gold-tipped ones to arouse burning desire, as in the story of Daphne and Apollo (see page 64). Back at the beginning of the cosmos, Eros makes it possible for primordial forces to mate and to bring forth new beings.

PERSONIFICATION OR DEITY?

Many Greek abstract nouns such as the words for peace, strife and wisdom are feminine in gender and so lend themselves to being portrayed as women. When Nike (Victory) settles on a ship in battle, is she an abstract noun or a goddess? Personifications are useful for grasping abstract concepts. For example, Tyche (Luck) is shown as a woman holding a rudder to steer people's lives, and a cornucopia full of things they will receive in this life. Eris (Strife) is shown as a woman with the golden apple that will cause the Trojan War. Abstract nouns are not always feminine in gender, however. Eros, the personification of sexual love, is masculine. The renowned art historian E.H. Gombrich observes that, if such personifications had a cult (i.e. were worshipped with altars and images), the ancient Greeks considered them divinities.

EREBUS, NYX, AETHER & HEMERA

Also out of Chaos come Erebus, a kind of personification of darkness, and black Nyx (Night). From them come the first things born from 'mixing in love': Aether (Upper Air) and Hemera (Day). The job of Nyx is to bring night, and that of her daughter Hemera to bring day. Nyx is sometimes shown as a winged female in a chariot. The famous head of an exhausted horse from the Parthenon's east pediment is thought to be pulling the chariot of Nyx (or possibly Selene, the moon). Nyx also gives birth to many personifications. Some are bad like Doom, Fate, Blame, Woe, Nemesis, Deceit, Old Age and Death (Thanatos). Others are neutral or even positive, like Sleep (Hypnos) or Friendship. Nyx also gives birth to the Fates (see page 130). Writing six centuries after Hesiod, the Roman statesman and philosopher Cicero makes Erebus and Nyx the parents of Eros. There is no canonical version of the Greek myths!

☞ Phaedra and Eros on a vase
*c.*345 BCE, British Museum

URANUS

Gaia (Earth), the second thing to come into existence, spontaneously brought forth Uranus (Sky) as her equal. There is a handy mnemonic link here. The Greek word for sky (*ouranos*) is linked to the Greek verb *oureo* 'to make water' in the sense of 'to rain' or 'to urinate'. So I remember that Uranus is Sky because he 'urinates' on Gaia. This is an obvious image of insemination. From the union of Uranus and Gaia come three sets of siblings: the Titans (see opposite), the three Cyclopes (not to be confused with the Cyclops from Homer's *Odyssey*) and also the three Hekatonkheires, or 'Hundred-handed Ones', each of whom also has 50 heads. Uranus either hated his offspring or was afraid of being deposed, a theme we see often in the myths, so he kept burying them in Gaia. This would prove to be a big mistake. In response, Gaia began shaping a great sickle made of flint (see page 106)…

COSMOLOGY

Even personified, the proto-gods and their offspring are confusing. It is hard to visualize them. Although Gaia (Earth) is sometimes shown as a woman, the ancient Greeks also pictured earth as a kind of discus floating upon a body of water (Oceanus) that looks like a doughnut-shaped stream. Above Gaia was Uranus (Sky); he was comprised of Aer, the lower atmosphere, and Aether, a brighter, lighter upper atmosphere.

Imagine a snow globe with a circular instead of an oval base. Instead of one clear dome above it, there are several, representing the different 'heavens'. But there is another mirror-image snow globe below it, this one black. First the are primeval waters, then the underworld, then Chaos and finally Tartarus, the lowest of the low, where many of the Titans are eventually imprisoned.

THE TITANS

The Titans were the most human-looking of the offspring of Gaia and Uranus. Hesiod names 12 of them in his *Theogony*, six female and six male. Notable among these were Oceanus, father of 3,000 sea nymphs (Oceanids); Themis, mother of the Seasons – the Horae – and the Fates – the Moirai (Hesiod seems be citing another tradition here as he elsewhere proposes Nyx as mother of the Fates); Mnemosyne, mother by Zeus of the nine Muses, and Iapetus, father of the second-generation Titans Prometheus, Epimetheus, Menoetius and Atlas. The most powerful first-generation Titan was the youngest one, Cronus. Hesiod describes him as crafty and terrible. He will mate with his Titan sister Rhea to produce the third generation of gods, the Olympians. As the new Olympians gained power, some of the Titans declared war on them. An extended battle ensued, the Titanomachy, lasting ten years. Zeus and his siblings were finally victorious and imprisoned most of the Titans in Tartarus, just as Cronus had done to his father Uranus (see page 106).

BATTLE OF GODS & GIANTS

A hugely popular subject of Greek art from the 6th century BCE was the Gigantomachy, the battle of Olympian gods and Gigantes (Giants). We don't know much about it since Hesiod and Homer never mention the battle although they do mention the Giants. The Gigantomachy is not the same as the Titanomachy although some ancient writers conflated the two.

Apollodorus, writing in the later Roman period, is our most complete source. He claims that Gaia gave birth to the Giants to get revenge on the Olympians for imprisoning the Titans. The Gigantomachy appears early in art, especially on Athenian vases, but also on sculptures. The most exciting can be found in Berlin, on a massive 2nd century BCE marble altar brought from Pergamum, an ancient Greek town in what is now Turkey. Although Apollodorus names some of the Giants, in the earliest depictions they resemble anonymous soldiers with swords and shields. Later, some of them get snaky legs.

One fun aspect of the depiction of the Gigantomachy on vases and in sculpture is the variety of bespoke weapons used against the Giants by the Olympians: Zeus has his thunderbolt, Hephaestus throws hot coals, Dionysus pokes with his thyrsus, Athena with her spear, Poseidon wields a trident and the island of Nisyros, Apollo and Artemis employ bow and arrows. The Giants were eventually buried under volcanoes such as Etna and Vesuvius, and so may be partly aetiological.

POWER
COUPLES

RHEA & CRONUS
(Roman OPS & SATURN)

Rhea was a Titaness, a child of Gaia and Uranus. Cronus was her younger brother, also a Titan. 'Crooked-minded' Cronus wanted power, so he castrated their father with a flint sickle made by his mother. Then he imprisoned Uranus in Tartarus and married Rhea. For a while they ruled happily over the second generation of gods. But Cronus was afraid he would be deposed by one of his children, as he had deposed his father. So every time Rhea gave birth he would swallow the baby. Rhea soon tired of this. When her sixth baby was born she hid him in Crete and gave Cronus a rock wrapped in swaddling clothes for him to swallow instead of the baby. The rescued baby was Zeus, and when he was old enough, he deposed his father, freed his swallowed siblings and took the throne.

Rhea then became a kind of divine grandmother, assisting her Olympian children when needed. For example, she helped Leto give birth to Apollo and she raised Dionysus. In Greek times, Rhea was sometimes confused with Gaia or Cybele. In Roman times, she was known as Magna Mater, the Great Mother. Today, Rhea is the largest moon orbiting the planet Saturn (the Roman name for Cronus). That might help you remember that they are a power couple, like Gaia and Uranus.

METIS & ZEUS

Metis was an Oceanid, one of the 3,000 daughters of Oceanus. But she was special. Her name means wisdom, cunning or skill, as in the cunning of a fox or the skill of a poet. Like her name, she was clever. It was her idea to give Cronus a special potion to make him vomit up Hera, Hestia, Demeter, Poseidon and Hades, plus the stone substituted for Zeus. As her reward, Zeus took her to bed. But then it was prophesied that her daughter would be wiser than her mother and her son would be greater than his father. Therefore, Zeus followed his father's example and swallowed Metis whole.

Metis, however, had already conceived. She moved from Zeus' stomach to his mind and there raised her daughter and crafted armour for her. Athena was born thanks to Hephaestus' axe. When he split Zeus' head open, out popped the goddess of wisdom, fully armed. But Metis continued to indwell Zeus, so one of his epithets is *Metieta* – 'All-Wise Counsellor' (*Iliad* 1.175). Sometimes, on vases showing Athena's birth, a female figure hides beneath his throne. She may represent Metis.

☞ Birth of Athena (with Metis) on
a drinking cup *c.*555 BCE, British Museum

107

PANDORA & EPIMETHEUS

Men always like to blame things on women. The oldest account of the first mortal woman is in *Theogony* by Hesiod, who was a grumpy misogynist. He tells how after Zeus punished Prometheus (see page 128) for bringing fire to humankind, he then punished humans for accepting the fire by giving an 'evil thing' to Epimetheus, the less clever brother of Prometheus. (Prometheus' name means 'foreknowledge' while Epimetheus' name means 'afterthought'.) The 'beautiful evil thing' gifted by Zeus to humankind (who were literally all men at that time) was the first woman, moulded by Hephaestus and dressed by Athena.

In his other didactic poem, *Works and Days*, Hesiod tells us the first woman's name was Pandora, which means 'all gifts'. However, not all the gifts were good. As instructed by Zeus, Hermes gave her lies, flattering words, a thievish heart and the ability to speak. Pandora and all her female descendants will be a blight to men, driving them into poverty. However, Zeus adds a rotten cherry on top by means of another gift to Epimetheus – a big storage jar with a lid, full of all the woes that will plague humankind: sickness, pain and death. This jar is the famous 'Pandora's Box'. Pandora removes the lid from the jar, possibly in all innocence, for the account does not say anyone told her not to (*Works and Days* 83ff.). As she lifts the lid, all the woes are released into the world. Only Hope is stuck under the lid.

But there is a problem here. If Hope is still in the jar, then humankind doesn't have it. But maybe Hope is a bad thing, like all the other woes. The Greek word for hope, *elpis*, could also mean expectation, dread or even foreknowledge. Knowing what will happen to us would make all those other woes even worse, so maybe it's for the best that Foreknowledge stayed stuck in the jar. Also, Epimetheus was warned by his wiser brother not to accept any gifts from Zeus. Like the story of Eve in the Garden of Eden, if we look more carefully, we see that the man is also to blame.

PYRRHA & DEUCALION

It's astonishing how many cultures have a story about a great flood. There are several in Hindu mythology, and the Native American Cheyenne people also have a flood story. Then there is the story of Noah and his family in the Hebrew Bible. In 1872, self-taught linguist George Smith was poring over ancient cuneiform tablets in the British Museum when he came across an account of a great flood in the Epic of Gilgamesh. When he realized that he was reading a flood story recorded centuries before the Hebrew version, he got so excited, a contemporary account tells us, that he 'jumped up and rushed about the room in a great state of excitement, and, to the astonishment of all those present, began to undress himself' (E.A. Wallis Budge, *The Rise and Progress of Assyriology*, page 153).

There is an ancient Greek flood tale, too. It has many elements in common with Noah's flood, including a man and a woman who must repopulate the Earth. Zeus is fed up with the evil and impious race of men and decides to wipe them out. At first, he thinks of using his thunderbolts, but then recalls that the universe is destined to be destroyed by fire at some later date, so he decides to use water. When he has covered the Earth with a combination of rain, rising tides and flooding rivers, he spots one man and one woman left, both innocent and worshipping the gods. These are Pyrrha and Deucalion. Pyrrha was the daughter of Pandora and Epimetheus. Deucalion, the son of Prometheus, has had the foresight to find a skiff for them to climb into and they land on top of Parnassus in central Greece, reduced by floodwaters to a little island. Zeus decides to spare them.

When the waters recede the couple weep, and Deucalion wonders if he can form new men of clay, the way his father did. The couple decide to enquire of an oracle and are told to unbelt their robes and throw the bones of their great mother behind them. Pyrrha finally solves the riddle: their 'mother's bones' are the 'stones of the Earth'. Half doubting that this could be the answer, they loosen their clothes and move downhill, throwing stones over their shoulders behind them. It works. Every stone thrown by Deucalion becomes a man and all those tossed by Pyrrha become women (Ovid, *Metamorphoses* 1.348ff.).

HARMONIA & CADMUS

Cadmus is possibly the earliest mortal hero of Greek mythology. A Phoenician from the city of Tyre, on the coast of what is now Lebanon, he lived in a time before even Perseus and Heracles. When Zeus abducted Cadmus' sister Europa, their father commanded Cadmus to bring her back or not to return. In Delphi, Cadmus consulted the oracle, who told him not to worry about his sister but to follow a heifer with a crescent moon shape on her flank and establish a city-state named Thebes where the cow lay down. This task also required him to kill a dragon sacred to Ares, god of war.

After Cadmus had achieved all this, Athena ordered Cadmus to sow the dragon's teeth. From them came a race of fierce warriors called Spartoi (not to be confused with Spartans) to populate the new city-state. Although Cadmus had been told to slay the dragon, he still had to do penance for killing a creature sacred to Ares. After eight years of serving Ares, he was given Harmonia (Harmony), the daughter of Aphrodite and Ares, as his bride. All the gods attended the wedding. Aphrodite's cuckolded husband, Hephaestus, gave the bride a beautiful necklace that secretly carried a curse.

According to some accounts, Cadmus and Harmonia eventually went to Illyria (modern Albania) where Cadmus became king. The curse of the sacred dragon still hung over them, and on their deaths they were changed into serpents, but not before Cadmus gave the Greeks a gift he had picked up in Phoenicia, the alphabet. The cursed descendants of Cadmus and Harmonia include: Semele, who was vaporized by Zeus' glory; Pentheus, who was torn to bits by his own mother in a Bacchic frenzy, and Oedipus, who unknowingly killed his father and married his mother. A best-selling book by the Italian writer Roberto Calasso, *The Marriage of Cadmus and Harmony* (1988), retells much of Greek mythology starting with Harmonia and her necklace.

🏺 Cadmus, the dragon and others on a vase *c.*355 BCE, Louvre

WHY THEBES?

The name Thebes is not as exciting as that of Troy, but it is a place packed with mythology and fascinating stories that pre-date the Trojan War. The Greeks believed it to be their oldest city-state, which it probably was. It was a city with high walls and seven gates that was often besieged and that suffered civil war between brothers.

Thebes was founded by Cadmus in Boeotia (pronounced bee-OH-sha), literally 'Cowland', at a spot where the prophesied cow lay down. Cadmus then married Harmonia, and they ruled there for a time. It was also the home of their daughter Semele (mother of Dionysus), Heracles (see page 143), Megara (his wife), Tiresias (a transgender prophet; see page 123), Pentheus (who met a sticky end), Jocasta (mother and wife of Oedipus), Oedipus (see page 153), Creon (a tyrannical ruler) and Antigone (see page 173).

The nearby city-state of Athens was a fierce rival of Thebes and many Athenian tragedians chose to project their anxieties onto the neighbouring city by setting their plays in Thebes. These include *The Bacchae* by Euripides; *Seven against Thebes* by Aeschylus; plus Sophocles' 'Three Theban Plays': *Oedipus the King*, *Oedipus at Colonus* and *Antigone*. You could say bad things always happen in Thebes.

PSYCHE & CUPID (Greek EROS)

This strange story, part allegory, is known to us from only one source, the 2nd-century CE Roman writer Apuleius (although depictions of Psyche and Cupid dating to before this are known). The author was a Numidian who spoke both Latin and Greek. He lived in many places, but in North Africa he was accused of witchcraft, specifically of making a rich woman fall in love with him and marry him. Apuleius wrote the only Latin novel to have survived complete – *The Metamorphoses*, more commonly known as *The Golden Ass*.

There are several stories recounted within the main story of *The Golden Ass*. One of them is that of Psyche, a girl so beautiful that people abandoned the shrines and altars of Venus to worship her instead. Furious, Venus sent her son Cupid to deal with her rival, but he fell in love with Psyche himself and whisked her off to his palace. He came to her at night, never letting himself be seen, and they enjoyed an idyllic marriage until

Psyche's sisters persuaded her to light an oil lamp to see what he looked like. For this betrayal Cupid banished Psyche from his presence. Eventually, they were reunited and lived happily ever after.

Because Psyche means 'butterfly' as well as 'soul', Psyche is often depicted with butterfly wings. And Cupid sometimes has his bird wings. Disturbingly to our modern sentiments, the couple are commonly depicted as children, possibly because Cupid is usually shown as a baby and Eros as an adolescent boy. How are Cupid and Psyche a power couple? They are found on many a sarcophagus, perhaps indicating that Love can save the Soul, a comfort for the bereaved.

☞ Marble Cupid kisses Psyche, 4th century CE, Ostia Antica Museum, Rome

PERSEPHONE & HADES
(Roman PROSERPINA & PLUTO)

The following scenario is all too common in Greek myths: a beautiful girl is engaged in innocent pleasures when a god spies her, grabs her and carries her off. Sadly, this probably echoed the fate of many girls living in conquered towns and cities. In this case, Persephone is a goddess, the daughter of Demeter and Zeus. Her name means 'Bringer of Death' and it has many variants in Greek writing and art: Persephonia, Persephatta, Pherrephassa, and – frequently in Athens – Pherrephatta, (as she is labelled on the drinking cup opposite).

One day, Persephone is picking flowers in a Sicilian field when her uncle Hades, god of the underworld, spots her and wants her. The earth cracks open and out he thunders in his infernal chariot, driven by black horses. He seizes her and plunges back into the chasm. While her mother Demeter searches for her, Persephone languishes in the dark and dreary underworld. She is so miserable that she refuses to eat. Demeter is also miserable and stops producing crops for humankind.

Just as she is about to be rescued by Demeter, Persephone is tricked by Hades into eating a a pomegranate seed. Because she has eaten food in the land of the dead, she is now required to spend a third of every year in the underworld. Up on earth, these months will be barren as Demeter mourns her absent daughter. However, like the girls seized by enemy warriors (Briseis in the *Iliad*, for example), Persephone becomes resigned to her fate and even comes to love her abductor. On Greek vases she is often shown dining peacefully with Hades. Sometimes they gaze lovingly into each other's eyes. These vases were often placed in graves and tombs, expressing hope that existence might not be all bad in the underworld.

Persephone and Hades on a drinking cup
*c.*430 BCE, British Museum

HOW MANY POMEGRANATE SEEDS?

Just before Demeter rescued Persephone from the underworld, Hades tricked her into staying with him for part of every year by coaxing her to eat some pomegranate seeds. Many people know a version of the story where Persephone eats six seeds and therefore has to remain in the underworld for six months out of every year. But, as with all the myths, each version varies. *The Homeric Hymn to Demeter* (6th century BCE) recounts that Hades gave her just one seed. In *Fasti* 4.607 (1st century BCE/CE), Ovid specifies three seeds. In *Bibliotheca* 1.5.3 (1st–2nd century CE), Apollodorus goes back to one seed. Only later do authors increase the number of seeds and make each seed equal a month.

EURYDICE & ORPHEUS

I can still remember when my mother read me the myth of Orpheus, a skilled musician who married a beautiful maiden named Eurydice. After the ceremony she was running in a grassy meadow when a snake bit her. And she died! Her husband Orpheus was so upset that he made the dangerous trip to the underworld to bring her back. Hades, king of the dead, and his lovely queen, Persephone, were moved by his music and told him he could take Eurydice back up as long as he didn't look back until they were in the sunny land of the living. But silly Orpheus looked back too soon, and his beloved Eurydice was lost to him for ever.

'But *why?*' the seven-year-old me protested. 'Why didn't he just wait a little longer? It's not fair!' Over 60 years later it still seems unfair. Orpheus' fatal error doesn't feel like hubris, but rather like a moment of doubt, caused by his passionate love for his wife. But after losing Eurydice for ever, he no longer had the desire to make music. This displeased the nymphs and girls who were used to his free lunchtime concerts. When he refused to play for them, they spitefully tore him to bits and tossed his limbs into a river. In some accounts, his head kept singing as it floated out to sea, although his soul was finally reunited with Eurydice.

GOLDEN TICKETS TO THE UNDERWORLD

Small tablets or gold metal leaves inscribed with instructions for the dead have been found in burial sites from the 4th century BCE in locations as varied as Thessaly, Crete, Egypt and Italy. They are often known today by the German word *Totenpässe* ('passports for the dead'). Usually written in Greek, they either tell the dead person what to say when standing before Hades or bear instructions for how to reach the best part of the underworld. Some are rectangular and others shaped like an ivy leaf. They can be rolled up and hidden in amulets, or placed in the mouth or on the chest.

These gold *lamellae*, or 'little tablets', could be linked to mystery cults such as those of Dionysus or Orpheus. One tablet from southern Italy tells the bearer not to drink from the spring by a white cypress tree, but to go farther down the path to the lake of Mnemosyne (Memory) and say to the guardians there, 'I am the child of Earth and starry Heaven. Give me water from this lake of memory, for I am dry with thirst.' If the 'subterranean queen' agrees, the soul can drink and continue on 'the sacred way with other initiates and bacchantes' (Hipponion tablet, *c.*400 BCE).

MEDEA & JASON

Jason, one of the few heroes born of two mortal parents, would probably not have succeeded on his quest to find the Golden Fleece without the help of a woman who was part goddess. Although he filled his ship, the *Argo*, with heroes (for more on Jason, see page 148), it was not a totally successful journey. When he arrives in Colchis at the far end of the Black Sea, the sorceress daughter of King Aeëtes falls in love with him. She is Medea, and she decides to betray her family and homeland for Jason. She gives him ointment to protect him from fire-breathing bulls, divulges the knack of overcoming warriors sprung from dragon's teeth and supplies him with a magic potion that puts the fleece-protecting dragon to sleep. When Jason seizes the fleece and they are all sailing away from Colchis, she even chops up her own brother and tosses the pieces in the sea to slow down her pursuing father.

Back in Jason's hometown, Iolcus, Medea gets rid of Jason's uncle, King Pelias, who sent the hero on the suicide mission in the first place, in a particularly nasty way. Having demonstrated her power by rejuvenating an old ram by cutting it up and throwing its parts into a cauldron, Medea tricks Pelias' daughters into carrying out the same procedure with their father – only he fails to survive. After ten years of marriage and two children, ungrateful Jason abandons Medea for a Corinthian princess. There are several versions of what happened next, but in a tragedy by Euripides, produced in 431 BCE for the City Dionysia festival, Medea gets revenge by murdering her own children by Jason. 'I know what I'm about to do is wrong,' says Medea at one point, 'but my ability to deliberate has been conquered by my fury.' Athenians were so shocked by this plot twist that the play took last place in the competition. But nobody could forget the horrific story, and today this version of events has become canon. *Medea* is one of the most highly regarded examples of Greek tragedy.

Medea rejuvenates a ram on a vase
*c.*480 BCE, British Museum

HOW PLAYWRIGHTS PLAY WITH MYTHS

Athenian playwrights used the myths and archetypal characters to comment on their own world, often changing or embellishing earlier versions. Some of their interpretations of the always fluid myths are so memorable that they have been frozen into canonical ice cubes. For example, in some early versions of Medea's story she does not kill her own children and even rejuvenates Jason when he grows old. However, after Euripides' *Medea*, she is always known and depicted as a filicide. Another tragedian, Aeschylus, may have got the idea that Oedipus killed his own father from the *Telegony*, a lost epic where Odysseus is killed by his son Telemachus. I once heard classicist Mary Beard say that retelling these stories is 'not creative laziness; it's squeezing the myths to make them work for all they've got.'

THETIS & PELEUS

These two are definitely a power couple. Thetis was a Nereid (a sea nymph daughter of Nereus, a son of Gaia). She had the ability to change her shape into any creature and she was very beautiful. All the gods desired her, but it had been prophesied that any son she bore would be greater than his father. Therefore, Zeus decreed that she must marry a mortal. The wise centaur Chiron told Peleus the secret of winning her hand. He had only to grab her and hold on tight, no matter what shape she assumed, be it fire, water or wild beast.

Peleus held on until Thetis gave into his proposal, and the pair were honoured with a wedding attended by all the gods. Unfortunately, one goddess was not invited: Eris (Strife). To get revenge she showed up anyway and tossed a golden apple into the banquet hall following the ceremony. Inscribed 'To the Most Beautiful', this apple would in time cause the Trojan War (see page 39). Meanwhile, back on the couple's wedding night, Achilles was conceived, later to become one of the greatest heroes of Greek mythology.

The so-called 'courtship' of Thetis and Peleus was a popular theme on vases. Peleus is shown with his arms around Thetis as she transforms into various creatures. One of the oldest depictions of the Olympian gods is on the so-called Sophilos Dinos in the British Museum, showing the celestial family arriving to celebrate the couple's wedding.

Peleus grasps shape-shifting Thetis on a vase *c.*510 BCE, British Museum

PATROCLUS & ACHILLES

The Song of Achilles by Madeline Miller became a best-selling novel in 2015. It proposes the idea that Achilles and his foster brother Patroclus were more than best friends: they were lovers. Homer, our oldest source, gives no hint of a sexual relationship, although he shows the extraordinary depth of their love for one another. He describes them sleeping in the same inner room, but each with a girl by his side (*Iliad* 9.663ff.).

Achilles bandages Patroclus on a drinking cup *c.*500 BCE, Berlin

However, by the Classical period a few centuries later, it was an accepted social custom for an older man to take an adolescent boy as his lover and protégé. The older man took the dominant role of *erastes*, the penetrator, and the boy took the passive role of *eromenos*, the one desired. Sometimes there was not even penetration but only intercrural intercourse, where the *erastes* rubbed his erect member between the thighs (*crura*) of the *eromenos*. So when Aeschylus has Achilles praise the thighs of Patroclus in his tragedy *Myrmidons*, he is strongly implying that they were lovers and that Achilles was the *erastes*. In Plato's *Symposium*, a discussion about love at a lively dinner party, one of the speakers proposes the pair as an example of divinely approved lovers and argues that Patroclus was the *erastes*. The question 'Were Achilles and Patroclus lovers?' has been discussed throughout the centuries and is just as popular today.

GENDER FLUIDITY

Although Graeco-Roman culture was a patriarchy, many Greek gods, goddesses and heroes are pansexual and a few exhibit gender fluidity. The myths are peppered with characters who were cross-dressers. Dionysus dressed as a girl when young, and the warrior Achilles was made to disguise himself as a girl, too. Athena often took the form of a man or youth when she interacted with mortals. The Romans were particularly fascinated by Hermaphroditus, the offspring of Hermes and Aphrodite, who merged with an amorous nymph to become a single person with breasts as well as male genitalia.

But the most famous example of gender fluidity must be Tiresias, a long-lived Theban prophet who transitioned from male to female and back again. The son of a shepherd and the nymph Chariclo, he saw two copulating snakes and hit them with a stick. Hera punished him by transforming him into a woman. He married, had children and when he saw another pair of snakes seven years later, he either left them alone or hit them again (depending on the version of the story) and was changed back into a man, but now blind and with the gift of prophecy. There are many versions and embellishments of his story, but my favourite is that, when asked which gender got more pleasure while making love, he stated that on a scale of one to ten, 'the men only receive a one, but the women score nine' (*Apollodorus* 3.6.7).

MISCELLANEOUS
DEITIES

Hesiod names more than two hundred deities apart from the 'Big Twelve', and there are probably a thousand if you look hard enough. Here are just a few of the more notable ones.

HEBE (Roman JUVENTAS)

Her name means 'Youth', and she is cupbearer to the gods (*Iliad* 4.2). But her parents are Zeus and Hera, so why doesn't she have a place in the pantheon and why is she only a cupbearer? She was important enough to make an appearance on two ancient and important artefacts, the Sophilos Dinos in London and the François Vase in Florence. Hesiod even names her before Ares: 'Finally, Zeus made Hera his blooming bride, and she lay with the king of gods and men, and she gave birth to Hebe and Ares and Eileithyia' (*Theogony* 921ff.). Eileithyia was important as the goddess of childbirth, despite her unspellable and unpronounceable name, but where is Hebe? She makes one appearance in the *Iliad* when she gets to bathe her dusty and bloody brother Ares (*Iliad* 5.905). And, according to the *Odyssey* (11.603), she ends up marrying the deified Heracles. And shrines to her have been found in Athens and Rome. So I suppose it's a case of the Hestia syndrome: she's too nice to have many exciting stories about her.

PAN (Roman FAUNUS)

Half-goat, half-man, Pan appears in Athenian art only after the Battle of Marathon in 490 BCE when he was supposed to have caused 'panic' (Pan-ic) among the Persians, thus helping the Athenians gain victory. Despite this late appearance, he may have been an extremely ancient god whose origins are lost in the mists of time. Some scholars think he became Hermes, while ancient mythographers make him the son of Hermes and a nymph named Dryope (or even of Hermes and Odysseus' otherwise faithful wife, Penelope!).

Pan was born with goat horns protruding from his forehead, pointy ears and goat's feet. He turned a nymph called Syrinx into his special instrument: panpipes. Being half-goat, he is highly sexed. A notorious sculpture from Pompeii shows Pan making love to a she-goat. But Pan is not choosy. He is ready to make love to any female: girls, maenads, nymphs and even the goddess Aphrodite, who is often shown playfully beating him off with a sandal. According to Plutarch, a sailor living during the reign of the Roman Emperor Tiberius heard a voice coming across the water, telling him to proclaim that 'the great god Pan is dead!' Tiberius ruled from 14 to 37 CE, at the time when Jesus taught and died. For this reason, many Christians consider the statement prophetic.

Because Pan is a creature of the wild, he can be either horrific or appealing, savage or innocent. Some psychiatrists equate him with the 'id', or 'pleasure principle', the part of the self that goes for what it wants without stopping to question motives. J.M. Barrie wrote *Peter Pan* as a play in 1904. The book, written in 1911, has an earthy subtext in keeping with the nature of Pan. Some readers see Pan in the character of Dickon from *The Secret Garden* (1911), by Frances Hodgson Burnett, where he is first seen sitting beneath a tree and playing pipes to entice wild animals to come to him. In *The Lion, the Witch and the Wardrobe* (1950), Mr Tumnus is not Pan but one of his followers, a faun. The author, C.S. Lewis, once said that the idea for the book came to him following a mental picture he had of a faun in the snow with umbrella and parcels.

☞ Hebe goes to a wedding on the Sophilos Dinos *c.*575 BCE, British Museum

PROMETHEUS

Son of the Titan Iapetus, Prometheus was also considered to be a Titan. According to some accounts, Prometheus helped Zeus make humankind. One of Aesop's Fables has him use special clay made of earth moistened with tears. Having thus developed affection for his creation, Prometheus taught humanity how to make a trick offering to Zeus. He cut up a bull, divided it in half and made two piles. In one pile he hid the bones under tasty fat and in the other he disguised choice cuts of meat beneath hairy hide and guts. Then he asked Zeus to choose which portion would be his and which kept by humankind. Zeus went along with the ruse but punished humanity by denying them fire, so they could not even burn the fragrant fat.

Going behind Zeus' back, Prometheus now smuggled fire to humankind. At that point humankind was made up of only men. Zeus punished them by sending them the first woman, Pandora (see page 108). But the king of the gods was even angrier at Prometheus and punished him in a terrible way. He pinned the Titan to a rock, like a butterfly to a cork board, and summoned an eagle to feast on his liver during the daytime. At night the liver grew back so Prometheus had to endure the same torment day after day. Because he was immortal, this might have gone on for ever. Thankfully, mythographers from Hesiod and Aeschylus to Diodorus Siculus bring him respite. Heracles comes across Prometheus on his way home from one of his Labours, kills the eagle and frees the Titan, with the permission of Zeus.

HECATE

The goddess Hecate is mentioned by Hesiod in his *Theogony* as the only divinity apart from the sun god Helios to witness the abduction of Persephone. She is associated with the moon, borders, thresholds and especially crossroads, and also with night, light, graves, ghosts, plants, herbs and dogs. She protects against witchcraft possibly because she herself is a witch. Her rites often involved dog sacrifices. She almost always holds a torch and sometimes she is shown in her threefold form as Hecate Trimorph, though often with just two heads in profile, because three are difficult to depict. She is the daughter of two Titans, and she uses her torch to help Demeter search for Persephone. Later she becomes Persephone's companion in the underworld. She is sometimes shown guiding Persephone back to the upper world, using a fourfold torch, which may have been an aspect of the Eleusinian Mysteries. She is a favourite with those who love witchcraft and the dark arts. Ancient Greeks sometimes made night-time offerings to her of moon-shaped cakes illuminated by candles. Could this be the origin of birthday cakes with candles?

Hecate with a fourfold torch on a vase *c.*360 BCE, British Museum

THE FATES (Roman PARCAE)

The Fates, who determine the lifespan of every mortal, are depicted as three women, usually old crones. They are also known as the Moirai, which means 'portions' in Greek. The word 'fate' comes from the Latin *fata*, 'prophetic words' or 'destiny', while their Roman name, Parcae, comes from the Greek root *plek*, related to twisting thread or weaving.

Hesiod gives us two different accounts of their birth (see pages 101 and 103) and is the first to tell us their names and jobs. Clotho spins out the thread of a person's life. Lachesis measures how long that thread will be. Atropos cuts the thread, thereby determining the length of life. In some accounts, the Fates also pronounce the character of the person whose life they are spinning. Only on rare occasions can they be overruled.

This trio of goddesses hardly ever appear on Greek vases. However, in 1978, a fragment of ancient Greek pottery some 5cm (2in) across was spotted in an art and antiquities gallery on Rodeo Drive in Beverly Hills California. It showed the profiles of three females and the Greek letter M. The piece has now been restored to its rightful place on the famous Sophilos Dinos in the British Museum where the M helps spell out MOIRAI. At last, the Fates can now attend the wedding of Peleus and Thetis along with the other gods.

☞ Fragment of the Sophilos Dinos with three profiles of the Moirai, *c.*575 BCE, British Museum

THE MUSES

We have all had the experience of an idea, story or song 'springing' into our heads, or of getting into a 'flow' during a creative activity. This form of inspiration was first personified by the Greeks as female divinities, the Muses. 'For nine nights Zeus the All-Wise slept with Mnemosyne,' Hesiod tells us, 'and she bore nine girls whose hearts and minds and carefree souls were passionate for singing' (*Theogony* 56ff.). Hesiod gives us their names and describes them actually dancing around a spring, a helpful visual metaphor of their method. They helped artists in the realm of music (a word we get from them): poets, musicians and dancers.

The Muses varied in number and function over the centuries, but Hesiod's nine became popular and eventually genres and attributes were assigned to them, often simply to match their names.

- Mnemosyne's name means 'memory'. Poets needed a prodigious memory as well as inspiration. She is not one of Hesiod's nine but rather their mother, one of the Titans.
- Clio ('glory') – muse of history. Sometimes shown with scrolls.
- Euterpe ('giving delight') – muse of elegiac poetry. She holds an aulos (double pipes).
- Thalia ('abundance') – muse of comedy/pastoral poetry. Comic mask and/or shepherd's crook.
- Melpomene ('singer') – muse of tragedy. Tragic mask.
- Terpsichore ('delights in dance') – muse of dance. Apollo's lyre.
- Erato ('desirable') – muse of love poetry. A cithara (a fancy kind of lyre).
- Polyhymnia ('many praises') – muse of songs for rite and ritual. A veil.
- Urania ('of the heavens') – muse of astronomy. A globe and compass.
- Calliope ('beautiful voiced') – muse of epic poetry. A writing tablet.

MITHRAS

This mysterious god is not the Persian god Mithra, but a kind of spin-off. He appears in the 1st century CE, around the time of the birth of Christianity. Both Mithraism and Christianity are types of mystery cult, teaching their followers how to obtain a better life in the next world. The cult of Mithras made the mistake of limiting followers to men. Christianity let in anybody, including women and children. Mithras himself is always shown in distinctive Persian dress from his floppy Smurf hat to his slippers. Especially 'barbaric' were his leggings and tunic with long sleeves.

The young god appears over and over in a very strange pose: kneeling on a bull with one leg bent and the other outstretched. His cape flutters behind as if in a strong wind, and he turns his head to look away as he stabs the bull in the shoulder. The term 'tauroctony', or 'bull-killing', has been applied to this image, but you cannot kill a bull by stabbing it in the shoulder; you can only disable it. Some scholars believe this is an apotropaic image to keep away evil. Sometimes this scene is encircled by the Zodiac, and two torchbearers may appear, one with a downward pointing torch (usually symbolizing death or night) and one with torch raised. One theory is that the torches point the way for the soul to go after death, either up to a holding pattern in the stars or down to the next body it will inhabit.

☞ Fresco of Mithras stabbing the bull, 2nd century CE, Capua

ISIS

Another popular non-Greek god was Isis. An import from Egypt, she was hugely popular in the Roman period and had a temple in Pompeii. Isis features as a *dea ex machina* at the end of Apuleius' *The Golden Ass* (see page 112). She also appears in a Roman-period account of the life of Aesop. According to the story, Aesop was an ugly enslaved person born in Phrygia (modern Turkey) with a speech impediment. One day, while working in the fields, Aesop spotted a passing priest of Isis. He shared his meagre lunch and fetched him water. Later, as Aesop napped under a tree, the goddess Isis herself appeared to him in a dream and rewarded him with the gift of eloquent speech. When Aesop woke, not only could he speak beautifully, but he could also understand the speech of animals. This ability led to his rise from enslaved person to philosopher.

MIX 'N' MATCH

The ever-adaptable Romans absorbed many of the Greek gods and made them their own. Romans already had a goddess like Artemis, so they added elements of her personality and mythology and called her Diana. The same applied to Ares, who became Mars; Hera who became Juno; Hestia who became Vesta, and so on. Only Apollo retains his Greek name, possibly because he is a 'new god' in comparison to older ones. Romans also took non-Greek gods and mixed them with their own, often to keep conquered peoples happy. One of the best known is Serapis, a mixture of Zeus and the Egyptian gods Osiris and Apis. Another is Sulis-Minerva, the goddess of the hot springs at Bath Spa in Britain. She is a conflation of the Roman goddess Minerva and the local deity Sulis. Mithras is also a 'mash-up' god (see opposite). This mixing of gods to make a new one is called 'syncretism'.

HEROES &
ANTI-HEROES

A hero is usually a demigod – that is, a man or woman who claims at least one divine parent and is therefore superior to ordinary humans in size, beauty and/or special powers. Some ancient heroes were venerated as ancestors or even worshipped at shrines. Many had Zeus as a father, but other gods and goddesses also begat heroes. Poseidon was the father of Theseus, for example, and Thetis the mother of Achilles.

A hero does not have to be morally good, and in fact most of the heroes from the Greek myths might better be called 'anti-heroes', lacking many of the qualities that the word 'hero' summons up today such as generosity, kindness, selflessness and compassion. Two very early anti-heroes are Sisyphus and Tantalus (see below and page 139).

Just as there are three generations of gods in Greek mythology, I like to divide heroes into roughly four generations. The Earliest Heroes would start with Cadmus and include Perseus, Bellerophon and Pelops right at the end. Then come the Hunter–Argonauts, heroes who sailed with the *Argo* and/or hunted the Calydonian Boar. These include Jason, Heracles, Orpheus, Peleus, Castor, Polydeuces (Pollux) and Atalanta. Third we have the Oedipids, my made-up word for Oedipus and his descendants. They include Atreus, Creon, Antigone and so on. Finally come the heroes of the Trojan War, featuring Achilles, Agamemnon, Menelaus, Diomedes, Odysseus and the two Ajaxes, together with their opponents Hector, Sarpedon, Penthesilea and so on. These four 'generations' comprise one of Hesiod's Five Ages of Man – the Heroic Age – 'a divine race of men called demigods, the race preceding our own...' (*Works and Days* 157ff.).

TANTALUS

Tantalus' crime was fairly horrible. In order to see whether the gods were really all-knowing, he invited them to a banquet and served them chopped-up bits of his son Pelops (see page 143). The gods pushed their plates away in disgust, all except for Demeter who was still so upset by the loss of her daughter Persephone that she distractedly nibbled part of the shoulder.

Tantalus was condemned to suffer a fate befitting his crime. He was sent to Tartarus and made to stand in a pool of water beneath a fruit tree. Every time thirsty Tantalus bent down to drink, the water drained away. Every time he reached up for a piece of fruit, the branch recoiled, denying him the food he so craved. From him we get the word 'tantalize', meaning to tempt without hope of gratification.

SISYPHUS

You might have heard of Sisyphus and his punishment. He was commanded to push a massive boulder up a hill only for it to roll down again, compelling him to repeat the task over and over until the end of time. But what was the crime that deserved such a terrible penalty? The answer is that he cheated Thanatos (Death) not once, but twice. The first time, when Thanatos came to chain him up, he expressed disbelief that such small chains would hold him and asked Thanatos to demonstrate on himself. Thanatos (obviously not the brightest personification in the cosmos) ended up trapping himself. Even people who wanted to die, such as horribly wounded soldiers or mangled chariot racers, could not expire until Ares came to unchain Thanatos.

Sisyphus' second scheme to outwit Death was much more convoluted and involved him really dying, asking his wife not to bury him, and then begging Persephone to send him back to the land of the living so he could punish his wife for not giving him a proper burial. Despite a few plot holes (for example, you can't cross the river Styx to see Persephone if you're not buried), this scheme also worked. Now the gods were really peeved. When they finally caught up with Sisyphus, they sent him to Tartarus, the darkest part of Hades, and made him roll the big rock.

The French philosopher Albert Camus famously wrote a long essay called *The Myth of Sisyphus* (1942) comparing the fate of the mythical trickster with the lot of modern humanity. It is true that many of us see the 'daily grind' as a Sisyphean labour, getting us nowhere. Camus concludes that this myth symbolizes the absurdity of life and that we can be happy by accepting our lot and by rejoicing in the task of forever rolling the boulder up the hill.

🏺 Sisyphus pushes his stone on a vase *c.*350 BCE, Naples

PERSEUS

Famous for killing Medusa and rescuing Andromeda, and now made famous by Rick Riordan's popular Percy Jackson and the Olympians book series for middle-grade readers (with film and TV versions), this hero was the son of a princess named Danaë and Zeus. King Acrisius of Argos loved his beautiful daughter Danaë very much, but when it was prophesied that he would die at the hand of her son, he locked her up. Zeus managed to spot her and gain access as a shower of gold, possibly the only time he disguised himself as an inanimate object for the purpose of seduction. When Acrisius learned that Danaë had given birth to baby Perseus, he put them both in a chest and sadly pushed it out to sea. (By leaving their death to the elements and/or gods he would not be guilty of murder.) The box washed up on an island where it was found by a kind fisherman. Several years later the king of the island spotted Danaë and desired her, but she was unwilling. With strong young Perseus as her defender, King Polydectes had no hope of seducing Danaë. So he sent Perseus on a mission to bring back the head of Medusa, the once beautiful but now hideous Gorgon whose stare could turn men and beasts to stone.

With Athena as his mentor and the help of gadgets from the gods – the winged shoes of Hermes, the invisible helmet of Hades, a mirrored shield from Athena, plus a sharp sickle and bag for the severed head – Perseus went on a Hero's Journey (see page 142). In a not very heroic but quite sensible manner, he killed Medusa while she was asleep, careful to look in his mirrored shield and not directly at her, just in case she woke up. With her head in a bag he was flying over Ethiopia when he spotted a beautiful girl chained to a rock and about to be devoured by a sea monster. 'Close your eyes!' he cried to the girl and, averting his own gaze, he held up Medusa's head and turned the sea monster to stone. The monster had been ravaging the land and Princess Andromeda had been chosen as a sacrifice to appease it. Perseus took Andromeda home (after gaining her consent) and arrived just in time to turn the evil king and his followers to stone, thus saving his mother. Danaë married the kind fisherman and they became the new king and queen.

Perseus now gave Medusa's head to his mentor, Athena, who put it on the front of her aegis (see page 32). He returned with his bride to Argos. All seemed well until one

☞ Perseus, Medusa and Hermes on a vase c.540 BCE, British Museum

day, at an athletic contest, Perseus threw a discus and the wind made it strike old King Acrisius. Thus the prophecy was fulfilled, and Perseus and Andromeda became king and queen of Argos.

There are many variants to the story, not least on vases where Hermes rather than Athena is Perseus' helper. Perseus with the head of Medusa was a very popular theme on Greek vases, possibly because the *gorgoneion* staring out at the viewer was apotropaic, that is, it kept evil away.

THE HERO'S JOURNEY

In 1977, Christopher Vogler, a Hollywood scriptwriter working for Disney, sent a memo to his pals. It was a template for writing a screenplay about a hero, based on Joseph Campbell's hugely popular book, *The Hero with a Thousand Faces*. Yes, that's right: a formula – a paint-by-numbers method of writing a story. And it went viral, or whatever the equivalent was in 1977. Later that year a movie called *Star Wars* came out using that very formula and showed how well it worked. Essentially, Vogler's theory, based on Campbell, was that every hero's quest story was essentially the same, only the details were different. And if you apply it to many of the stories that follow you will see it in action.

One of the basic 'beats' is a 'call to adventure', when a herald figure sends the hero on a quest. If the hero 'refuses the call', then a 'mentor' encourages them and gives them a 'talisman'. The hero often crosses a threshold into the 'world of adventure'. Here they meet 'allies and opponents' and often undergo 'tests and trials'. All these combine to help the hero fulfil their potential.

Roughly halfway through the Hero's Journey comes the 'visit to death' beat, when the hero faces their mortality or literally visits the underworld. Around this time comes the 'final battle' and the 'grasping of the elixir' or 'gaining the prize'. Then the hero must undergo a kind of resurrection and make their way back home, having learned enough to fulfil their potential. If they learn too late – or not at all – it is a tragedy.

When I teach story structure to children, I tell them about Jason, Perseus, Heracles, Orpheus, Persephone and Aeneas. I cite classic films that hit these beats including *The Wizard of Oz* (1933), *The Matrix* (1999), *Harry Potter and the Philosopher's Stone* (2001), *WALL·E* (2008), *The Hunger Games* (2012), *Paddington* (2014) and many others.

PELOPS

One of the earliest heroes is Pelops, whose name means 'dark face' or perhaps 'dark eyes'. His lineage is confused but, according to Apollodorus (*Epitome* 2.3ff.), he was the son of Tantalus, who chopped him up, boiled him in a cauldron and served him to the gods at a feast. The gods punished Tantalus (see page 137) and managed to reconstitute and revive young Pelops, all except for his shoulder, which grieving Demeter had absent-mindedly eaten. For this he got an ivory replacement.

As an extremely handsome youth, Pelops was the lover of Poseidon, who gave him a special chariot. Pelops used this chariot in a race to win the hand of the princess Hippodameia. But he cheated and, as a result, he and his descendants were cursed. His kingdom soon grew to comprise the area of Greece subsequently known as the Peloponnese, or 'Island of Pelops'. As the father of Atreus, he was the grandfather of Agamemnon and Menelaus, key figures of the Trojan War, whose lives were to be blighted by the curse.

HERACLES (Roman HERCULES)

Heracles is a fascinating character. He is almost always shown wearing the skin of the lion he throttled as the first of his Twelve Tasks. Wearing the head as a hood makes him look part-human, part-animal. He wields a club (a caveman's weapon) along with a bow and arrow, another 'uncivilized' weapon usually associated with barbarians (a derogatory term for non-Greeks whose languages sounded as if they were saying 'bar-bar-bar').

Although born in Thebes, Heracles gets all over the Mediterranean. In Italy, he gives his name to Herculaneum, the city at the foot of Vesuvius. And legend has it he founded Pompeii, through which he led a procession (*pompa*) of cattle. Heracles is a civilizing influence, getting rid of monsters and helping ordinary mortals. He wrestles Thanatos (Death) to save the life of Alcestis (see page 172) simply out of the goodness of his heart.

However, Heracles can also tip over into berserker behaviour, especially when goaded by his jealous divine enemy, Hera. She hated him simply because he was the result of her husband Zeus' infidelity. (He was even given the name Heracles, which means 'glory of Hera', in an attempt to appease her, but it didn't work.) Heracles was such a popular hero that he was eventually deified and worshipped as a demigod. He has hundreds of adventures attached to him, set in many places and with many variations, but he is best known for his Twelve Labours, or Tasks (the word in Greek is *athlos*, 'contest for a prize', from which we get the word 'athletics'). After jealous Hera drove him to kill his wife and children in a temporary madness, the Delphic oracle told him he could achieve atonement and immortality if he completed certain tasks for his cousin Eurystheus, king of Mycenae. Many storytellers have riffed on versions of his Twelve Labours, from Agatha Christie's *The Labours of Hercules* (1947, with detective Hercule Poirot) to my own *Twelve Tasks of Flavia Gemina* (2003). And, of course, there is the 1997 Disney musical cartoon *Hercules*, beloved by many classical scholars.

Below and opposite are condensed versions of the tasks in the order given to us by our most complete source (Apollodorus, *Bibliotheca* 2.5.1ff.).

THE TWELVE TASKS OF HERACLES

1. Nemean Lion – a terrible lion was ravaging the countryside near Nemea. Because its golden hide was impervious to weapons, Heracles throttled it with his arm around its neck. He then used its own claw to skin it so he could wear it as a protective lionskin cloak.

2. Lernaean Hydra – how do you kill a monster who grows two new snaky heads for every one you club? Get your nephew (Iolaus) to cauterize each stump the moment you knock off a head.

3. Ceryneian Deer – sacred to Artemis and swifter than an arrow, Heracles caught it by dropping a net onto it while it slept. As he handed it over to Eurystheus, he let it speed away 'accidentally on purpose'.

4. Erymanthian Boar – a monstrous boar roamed Mount Erymanthos. Heracles drove it into hard-packed snow and bound the

half-frozen creature. When he carried it back to Eurystheus, still alive, the king was so frightened that he jumped into a giant *pithos* (storage jar).

5. Augean Stables – Augeas was the king of Elis and owner of 3,000 immortal cattle. The humiliating job of cleaning dung accumulated over dozens of years was cleverly achieved by diverting two rivers to wash it all away. Augeas had promised Heracles a tenth of his cattle as reward, but failed to honour the promise. Our hot-headed hero duly killed him.

6. Stymphalian Birds – at Lake Stymphalia in Arcadia, fierce birds were ravaging the crops. Heracles used bronze castanets (crafted by Hephaestus and gifted by Athena) to make the birds fly up so he could shoot them with his bow and arrows.

7. Cretan Bull – Heracles sailed to Crete and captured the magnificent bull who had fathered the Minotaur. After bringing it to Eurystheus, he set it free to roam Greece.

8. Mares of Diomedes – Diomedes, a Thracian son of Ares, owned four man-eating mares. During the task Abderus, a son of Hermes, went to help his lover, Heracles, but the horses killed him. Heracles fed Diomedes to his own horses and founded a town named Abdera in memory of his boyfriend.

9. Girdle of Hippolyta – after sailing with some pals to the southern Black Sea, to a land of female warriors called Amazons, Heracles politely asked their queen, Hippolyta, if he could borrow her girdle. This was not the sexy girdle worn by Aphrodite (see page 38) but a *zōstēr*, a warrior's belt. Hippolyta agreed but then Hera disguised herself as an Amazon and made everyone fight.

10. Cattle of Geryon – a giant with three bodies named Geryon lived on a remote island where Europe met Africa (i.e. off the southern tip of Spain) and owned a herd of fabulous red cattle. Heracles killed him with an arrow tipped with the poisonous blood of the Hydra. The trickier part was driving the cattle all the way back to Mycenae!

11. Golden Apples of the Hesperides – Heracles had to journey to the limits of the known world. The Hesperides were three nymph daughters of Atlas whose name means 'of the west'. In their garden was a tree with golden apples. Heracles temporarily took the heavens on his shoulders so their father, Atlas, could fetch the apples for him.

12. Cerberus – the final task of Heracles involved a literal 'visit to death' (see The Hero's Journey, page 142) to bring back Cerberus (see page 193). Heracles was initiated into the Eleusinian Mysteries so he could learn the way to Hades. The god of the underworld said he could borrow Cerberus if he could overcome him without weapons, which he did. A popular scene on vases is Heracles bringing the three-headed hellhound to Eurystheus, once again shown cringing in his *pithos*.

Heracles and Cerberus on a vase
*c.*525 BCE, Louvre

ORPHEUS

Born in Thrace to the Muse Calliope and the Thracian king Oeagrus, Orpheus is often shown wearing a floppy Phrygian Smurf hat. His superpower was music. By playing the lyre and singing poems of his own composition, he could charm mortals, animals, trees, nymphs and even gods.

Orpheus has a rich mythology. He helped Jason and the Argonauts safely pass the Island of the Sirens by playing his music to drown out their beautiful but deadly song. Later, after failing to bring Eurydice back from Hades (see page 116), Orpheus was so sad that he refused to play for the nymphs and they tore him limb from limb, like mad maenads. Another account says that, after Eurydice, he renounced women and was the first to turn his affections to young boys, which is why the nymphs killed him. There are several famous paintings of nymphs finding or holding the dismembered but still-singing head of the young musician.

STARS IN THE SKY

Many stars in the night sky immortalize Greek heroes, monsters and myths. Becoming a constellation was sometimes a consolation prize for heroes who suffered and died, such as Orpheus (represented by Lyra, his lyre), or Callisto and her son Arcas (see page 69). A few notable constellations are creatures from the tasks of Heracles: Leo the Nemean Lion, Taurus the Cretan Bull, Hydra the Serpent-headed Monster and Cancer the Crab (who tried to help defend the Hydra). Depictions of the constellations are rare in Greek art, but a charming 5th-century BCE amphora from Campania in southern Italy shows Heracles holding up the sky for Atlas; the heavens are represented by a bowl adorned with a crescent moon and two stars.

After he died, Orpheus became a psychopomp, someone who guides souls to the underworld. Like Dionysus, he got his own mystery cult, and in the 4th century BCE a collection of poems called the *Orphic Hymns* was named after him. His lyre was carried up to the dome of heaven by the Muses and is now the constellation Lyra.

☞ TOP: An angry female pursues Orpheus on a vase *c.*470 BCE, British Museum

☞ BOTTOM: Jason reaches for the golden fleece on a vase *c.*465 BCE, New York

JASON

Jason was one of those rare heroes who did not have a divine parent, though according to some accounts he was raised in a cave on Mount Pelion by Chiron the centaur. Hearing that his uncle Pelias has claimed his throne, Jason sets off home. On the way, he helps an old lady cross a river and, in so doing, he loses a sandal. The old lady is Hera in disguise, a rare instance where the ox-eyed queen of the gods doesn't hinder a hero. When Pelias sees Jason he is horrified because a prophecy has predicted that he would be overthrown by a man wearing one sandal. In order to avoid the blood guilt of murdering him, Pelias sends Jason on an 'impossible' mission, to get the Golden Fleece from distant Colchis, at the eastern end of the Black Sea.

As told in the 3rd-century BCE epic *Argonautica* by Apollonius of Rhodes, Jason gathers the biggest, baddest, buffest heroes to sail with him on his ship, the *Argo*. Along the way they have many adventures and, I have to say, a few misadventures. One such time is where they meet a friendly race of people who wine and dine them and even share around their single girls. The Argonauts sail off happily, but that night a storm catches them and blows them to a strange shore. They disembark and are attacked by the locals. In the darkness they fight back, only to discover they have landed in the same place from which they had departed and have just killed all their hosts of the previous day, who thought they were pirates. At least the Argonauts achieve a happy ending for Phineas, an ornery prophet plagued by unpleasant bird-women called Harpies (see page189).

Jason gets the Golden Fleece with the help of a princess sorceress named Medea (see page 118), but dumps her after ten years. In old age, he sits beneath the *Argo* dreaming of better times until one day a piece of the famous vessel drops off and kills him. Robert Graves wrote an interesting take on Jason's voyage in his novel *The Golden Fleece* (1944).

THESEUS

Theseus has fallen out of favour recently, probably because he treated women very badly. Plutarch lists all the women Theseus 'married' and it comes to nearly ten. The mother of this cancelled hero was called Aethra and she lived in the small town of Troezen near Corinth. One night she goes wading in the sea when Poseidon impregnates her. That same night Aegeus, king of Athens, also spends the night with her. Aegeus leaves his

☞ Aethra shows Theseus the talisman (sword and sandals) on a clay plaque,
1st century BCE – 1st century CE, British Museum

THE SHIP OF THESEUS PARADOX

There was a fun 'thought experiment' in ancient times centring around an ancient artefact.
After Theseus killed the Minotaur, he returned to Athens with the rescued youths. The
30-oared galley on which they sailed was preserved by the grateful Athenians who diligently
replaced the timbers as they rotted. According to Plutarch (*Theseus* 23.1), ancient philoso-
phers debated whether it was the same vessel after all the planks had been replaced. Today,
biologists claim that every seven years all the cells of our bodies have been replaced, just like
the planks of the Ship of Theseus. Some of us lose teeth or hair or even limbs. Some grow or
shrink in size or height. We are not what we were before. And yet we are.

sword and sandals under a massive rock. When Theseus is old enough to lift the stone and get these tokens, he sets off to Athens to claim his birthright, vanquishing robbers and villains along the way.

Arriving in Athens he approaches his mortal father Aegeus who is now married to Jason's ex, Medea. Seeing this strong young man as a threat, she warns Aegeus he might be an enemy and she prepares a poisoned drink. As Theseus lifts the deadly cup to his mouth, Aegeus spots his own sword and sandals and dashes the cup from Theseus' hand. Soon after, Theseus learns that every few years a tribute of seven girls and seven youths are sent from Athens to Crete to be sacrificed to the Minotaur, the monstrous half-bull, half-human offspring of King Minos' wife, Pasiphaë, and he promptly volunteers to be one of the young men. He promises his father that, if successful, he will return showing a white sail, rather than the black one he departs with.

As soon as Theseus and the other Athenian teens arrive in Crete, the daughter of King Minos falls in love with him. Princess Ariadne promises to help Theseus if he will marry her and take her home with him to Athens. Theseus agrees and she smuggles him a sword and – more importantly – a ball of wool so he can find his way out of the labyrinth, a maze beneath the royal palace where Pasiphaë's shameful offspring is hidden away. Theseus is victorious. He sails away with Ariadne and the other Athenian girls and boys.

Then Theseus does an unforgivable thing: he abandons Ariadne on the island of Naxos. He also forgets to change his sails from dark to light, causing his father to jump to his death into the sea, from then on known as the Aegean. The death of Aegeus proves handy because Theseus is now king of Athens. He has a disastrous marriage to Ariadne's younger sister, Phaedra, who develops a passion for his son Hippolytus (born to him by the Amazon Hippolyta). When Hippolytus rejects Phaedra, she hangs herself and leaves a note claiming he raped her. Theseus calls on his divine father Poseidon to kill Hippolytus. Poseidon sends a bull from the sea and causes Hippolytus' chariot to crash.

Left without offspring and now an old man, Theseus and his pal Pirithous (a very bad influence) decide to marry daughters of Zeus. First they go to Sparta and abduct Helen. She is only ten or twelve but her beauty is already renowned. Theseus stashes her away with his mother in Troezen until she can reach marriageable age. Then he and Pirithous make a journey to the underworld to get Persephone for Pirithous. Hades is not fooled and invites them to sit, but the chairs hold fast to their buttocks. Pirithous is left in the underworld, unable to rise and presumably unable to die. Theseus manages to pull away, leaving part of his buttocks on the chair. Athenians claim to this day that this is why most of their men have slim bottoms.

Mary Renault wrote two historical novels about Theseus, *The King Must Die* (1958) and *The Bull from the Sea* (1962), that show the hero in a more sympathetic light.

SPELLING & PRONUNCIATION

Spellings and pronunciations of the Greek deities are notoriously tricky. Is Demeter pronounced d-MEE-ter or DE-me-ter? Is the primal sky god Kronos, Cronos or Cronus? Not even scholars can agree.

PELEUS

If you ask most classicists who Peleus was, they will quickly tell you that he was the father of Achilles, the great hero of the Trojan War. If pressed for more facts, they might remember he won the hand of the sea nymph Thetis by ambushing her on the beach one day and then hanging on tight as she morphed through a succession of changes (see page 121). They might also remember that he sailed on the *Argo* with Jason and went on the hunt for the Calydonian Boar. He also had several wives before Thetis, but those marriages didn't work out.

That's all you really need to know about him, but if you want to impress myth lovers, tell them this: Peleus was the king of hard-to-pronounce Phthia – FTHEE-ya – in Thessaly (northern Greece).

CASTOR & POLYDEUCES (POLLUX)

As we saw on page 15, Zeus came to Leda in the form of a swan and impregnated her. In some versions of the myth, Leda produces two eggs. From one egg emerge an ordinary boy and girl, Castor and Clytemnestra. This is because Leda's husband Tyndareus also slept with her on the day of Zeus' seduction. From the other egg come Polydeuces and Helen, half divine, because they are from Zeus' seed. The brothers travel with Jason on the *Argo* (page 148). Although Polydeuces is half divine, Homer makes both the brothers mortal; they die fighting in the Trojan War (*Iliad* 3.235ff.). In the *Odyssey*, they get to live on alternate days, which seems fair, if disruptive. They are finally joined together forever in the constellation Gemini, the Twins, which commemorates them.

GREEKS OR ACHAEANS?

Greece did not exist as a unified concept in the Bronze and Iron Ages. Rather, it was a conglomeration of city-states linked by a common language, Greek (although there were many dialects). Homer uses the blanket term 'Achaeans' to describe the Greeks. Later, Herodotus divided the Greeks into four major tribes: the Achaeans (originally from the north-west Peloponnese), the Aeolians (islanders previously called the Pelasgians), the Ionians (from western Turkey and the Dorians (from mainland Greece). The Hellenes, a tribe from Thessaly, eventually gave their name to all Greeks and the word still used by modern Greeks to self-identify is 'Hellenes'. Finally, we get the English word 'Greeks' from the Romans, who got their Latin word *Graeci* from the Graikoi, a small tribe from Thessaly. Confused? We all are. That's why most English translations just stick with Greeks.

OEDIPUS

Just because he killed his father and married his own mother doesn't really make him a bad guy. He is just cursed (see Harmonia & Cadmus, page 111). His parents were warned that he would bring disaster on their house so they decided to expose him on a mountain (so they would not be technically guilty of his murder.) This ploy did not work with Paris or any other hero, and it doesn't work with Oedipus. In some accounts his father, Laius, even pierced his little ankles and tied them together so he could not crawl. But this sadistic detail might have been added to explain his name, which means 'swollen foot'.

Faithful to the trope, a shepherd finds baby Oedipus and brings him to the king and queen of Corinth, who long for a child of their own. They raise Oedipus as their son, not telling him the truth. This is a big mistake because, when he is grown up, Oedipus learns from the oracle at Delphi that he is destined to kill his father and marry his mother. Wanting to put as much distance as he can between himself and his 'parents', he decides never to return 'home' and instead heads for the nearest city. In an early instance of road rage, he kills a man at a crossroads, then carries on to Thebes where he learns that the king has just died and the city is in trouble.

A terrible half-woman, half-lion creature called the Sphinx is ravaging it and will not leave until someone solves her impossible riddle: What creature that speaks with one voice walks on all fours in the morning, on two feet during the day, and on three at night? Oedipus correctly guesses the answer is a human, who crawls in the morning of their life, walks on two feet for most of their days but uses a walking stick in their twilight years. The Sphinx self-destructs in rage and grateful Queen Jocasta offers to marry the handsome stranger who saved her city.

Several years and four children later a terrible plague strikes. Oedipus, whom some have called 'the first detective', decides to solve the mystery. The truth when he finds it is so horrible that Jocasta hangs herself and Oedipus puts out his own eyes. There are many variations and spin-offs of this story, including Sophocles' famous 'Three Theban Plays', one of which is the most popular Greek play of modern times, *Antigone*. And, of course, Sigmund Freud named a whole psychological complex after Oedipus.

ACHILLES

Achilles introduces us to the generation of heroes who fought in the Trojan War. The *Iliad*, one of the most important stories of Western civilization, and one of the oldest, was composed in the mists of the Bronze Age. At first it was recited, the metre and repetitive phrases helping performers remember all 16,000 lines. The Greeks got an alphabet from the Phoenicians around the year 750 BCE but the *Iliad* was not written down until about 700 BCE, by a person (or persons) who we call Homer. The epic's name (Greek *iliados*) means 'about Ilium'. Ilium was an ancient name for Troy, a citadel in what the ancient Greeks called Asia and we call Turkey.

Achilles fights Hector on a vase *c.*475 BCE, British Museum

But the epic poem is not really about the Greeks besieging Troy in order to avenge the kidnap of Helen of Sparta. The *Iliad* is about the anger of one Greek soldier, a half-god, half-human warrior named Achilles. A more accurate title might be something like 'The Anger of Achilles'. In fact, the very first word of the epic poem is 'rage'. First, Achilles is angry because he has been dishonoured by the leader of the Greeks, Agamemnon (see page 156), who has taken one of Achilles' prizes (a girl) when he had to give back one of his own prizes (another girl). For most of the poem Achilles sulks furiously in his quarters, but when his dear friend and companion Patroclus is killed, he finally emerges to slaughter many Trojans. It is not until the final book of the *Iliad* that he is calmed by the aged Priam, king of Troy. 'Pity me, Achilles,' Priam says. 'Remember your own father. I am more to be pitied than he because I dared to do what no human has ever dared. I pressed my lips to the hands of the man who killed my child' (*Iliad* 24.503ff.).

For many centuries this epic poem formed the core curriculum of children (mainly boys) growing up in ancient Greece and Rome. It was also my first proper introduction to Classics. I read E.V. Rieu's translation when I was 19, on my gap year, and was amazed. I could not believe that something composed so long ago could feel so modern. I was especially struck by a scene where the goddesses Athena and Hera were exchanging acid comments with each other like women in a beauty salon. (And this in a story about warfare!) A few months later I signed up for a class in Ancient Greek at university, and I was hooked on Classics for life.

One interesting fact about Achilles: the story of him being invulnerable apart from his heel comes very late, in the Roman period. It is told by Statius in his unfinished epic the *Achilleid*, written at the end of the 1st century CE. The expression 'Achilles' heel' has come to stand for someone's weakness or 'fatal flaw', and the Achilles tendon is so called after the most vulnerable part of this hero's body.

AGAMEMNON

The *Iliad* begins with a single long sentence in Greek that I have put into several English sentences:

> *Rage! Sing about the rage of Achilles, Goddess: the destructive rage of the son of Peleus, which pierced many Greeks with pain and sent many brave souls to Hades, making their bodies dinner for dogs and all the birds of prey. Start from the time when those two heroes first split in anger: the son of Atreides, Agamemnon, Lord of Men and godlike Achilles (Iliad 1.1–7)*

That sentence sets up our hero Achilles and Agamemnon as his opponent, which is immediately a shock as they are on the same side, fighting against the Trojans. Only later will Achilles' rage be turned on another opponent, Hector, who is a Trojan.

Although Achilles is the most feared warrior, Agamemnon is top dog. As leader and representative of the Achaeans he had agreed to sacrifice his eldest daughter, Iphigenia, to appease the gods and obtain the winds needed to blow the fleet to Troy. He survives the ten-year war and rashly returns home with a girl among his booty, the prophetess Cassandra. But his wife, Clytemnestra, Helen's sister, has already decided to punish him for killing their daughter. She slaughters him in the bath and in some accounts goes on to mutilate his body so that he will suffer dishonour even in the underworld. It is partly because of this mutilation that his son Orestes must avenge him...by killing Clytemnestra, his own mother. Athenian tragedians loved this story.

Agamemnon's ghost makes a cameo appearance in the last book of Homer's *Odyssey*.

LEARNING ANCIENT LANGUAGES

When I signed up for a beginner's class in Ancient Greek at the University of California, Berkeley in 1974, our teacher was a brilliant professor named W. Gerson Rabinowitz who sat in a permanent cloud of cigarette smoke and growled at us, asking us to 'parse' various sentences, that is, to dissect them grammatically. We were terrified and thrilled in equal measure. At first, the Greek text seemed to me like black worms crawling on white paper. But then the worms became letters and formed words, each one a window into the hot, thyme-scented world of ancient Greece. I had always loved the myths, but now I could see and hear and smell the people moving within them. I still find this every time I translate a passage of Greek, Latin or biblical Hebrew. Sometimes a single word can conjure an entire scene complete with sights, smells, sounds, movement and the feel of things.

HECTOR

The great hero of Troy, Hector, is King Priam's eldest son, described with several epithets: 'Tamer of Horses', 'Man-Killing' and 'Of the Glittering Helmet'. Although he does not approve of the war with the Greeks, he is the greatest warrior of the Trojans and therefore the main opponent of Achilles, at least on the battlefield. Unlike Achilles, he is not half divine, but mortal. He is depicted with nuance and sympathy, and is in many ways more admirable than Achilles. One of the most famous scenes in the *Iliad* is his meeting with his wife Andromache and little son Astyanax just inside one of the gates of Troy. He has momentarily left the battle to ask the women of Troy to pray hard and goes to see his wife, possibly for the last time. He finds her by the city gate with their little boy and a nursemaid. As they speak together, Andromache reminds him of how Achilles killed her father and all seven of her brothers in a single day, and how her mother died shortly thereafter. 'Hector,' she says, 'to me you are father and mother and brother and husband' (*Iliad* 6.429ff.). She begs him to stay and not to fight, because he will surely die. Hector cannot do this, because for men of his status dishonour is worse than death, and he has 'learned to be brave'.

In the same scene, Hector predicts what will happen to Andromache after his death, how a bronze-clad Achaean will lead her to a life of slavery, where she must work at a loom or carry water. 'May I be dead and deeply buried rather than hear your screams as they drag you into captivity,' he says (*Iliad* 6.464ff.). Hector reaches out to embrace his little boy:

> *Dazzling Hector stretched out his arms to take the boy, who shrank back crying into the arms of his comfortable nurse. He was frightened by the sight of his father in his bronze helmet with the terrifying horse-hair crest nodding down at him. At that his loving father and noble mother laughed out loud. Immediately, Hector took off the helmet and placed it on the ground. Then he kissed his precious son and swung him in his arms.* (*Iliad* 6.466ff.)

This is rightly one of the most famous passages in the epic. It is a moment of relief among so much tension and tragedy. But it is also an intensely sensory moment. The nodding crest paints a whole scene. It reminds us that Hector is clad head to toe in glittering bronze, probably smelling of sweat and dust and blood. Then we hear the wail of baby

Astyanax and the laughter of his parents, which relieves tension for us as well as for them. When Hector swings his toddler son, a thing every parent in the world has done, it triggers muscle memory and the powerful emotions that go with it. We can empathize.

But the very next moment we are reminded that they are not quite like us when Hector prays to Zeus and the other gods that this little boy will one day 'present the blood-spattered armour of his slaughtered enemy to delight his mother's heart' (*Iliad* 6.476ff.). This scene is even more poignant because Astyanax will not survive the sack of Troy (see page 163).

Andromache, Astyanax and Hector on a
vase *c.*365 BCE, Museo Nazionale, Ruvo di Puglia

ODYSSEUS

Odysseus is like Marmite – you either love him or hate him. He is a liar par excellence. He fought and schemed in the Trojan War for ten years, driving one on his own side to suicide, killing a Trojan spy cold-blooded, and finally gaining victory for the Greeks by trickery, with the famous Trojan Horse, a giant wooden equine full of armed men. Homer's other masterpiece, the *Odyssey*, tells how he spent ten leisurely years making his way home, living with some beautiful nymphs along the way and losing every single one of the men travelling with him. When he finally reaches Ithaca after a 20-year absence and meets a divine-looking stranger, does he tell them who he is? No, he does not. He spins a lengthy tale about being a Cretan merchant. The stranger is Athena, who grins and shakes her head and says, 'That's what I like about you, Odysseus; you're a big schemer like me.' When he returns to his palace, his old dog Argus recognizes him, wags his tail and whimpers. Does Odysseus give him a pat? No, he does not. And Argus dies.

When Odysseus comes face to face with his long-suffering wife Penelope, it (apparently) takes some convincing before she accepts that he is her husband. He slaughters all the men who have been hanging around his palace hoping to marry her, has the servant women hanged and then goes to reveal himself to his father, but not before spinning another lie about his identity. The epic poem ends with Odysseus fighting relatives of the slaughtered suitors until Athena calls a halt to the conflict. Eventually, he will go off on another journey – this was the story told in the lost epic called the Telegony.

Odysseus hides under a ram on a drinking cup,
6th century BCE, Cambridge

THE EPIC CYCLE

Alongside the *Iliad* and the *Odyssey*, there were once several other epic poems that told the extended story of the Trojan War. We have enough fragments and references to know roughly what happened. The whole cycle is as follows:

Cypria – the events leading to the Trojan War including the Judgement of Paris

Iliad – Achilles' anger and the death of the Trojan hero Hector

Aethiopis – the deaths of Penthesilea the Amazon, Memnon the Ethiopian and Achilles

Little Iliad – the construction of the Trojan Horse and contest for the arms of Achilles

Iliupersis – the destruction and sack of Troy

Nostoi – the return home of the Greek heroes Menelaus, Agamemnon and others

Odyssey – the return home of Odysseus

Telegony – the further adventures of Odysseus in which he sails to other lands and is eventually killed by his son Telegonus (by Circe) after his return

NEOPTOLEMUS

There are many other men, gods and heroes who do despicable things, but Neoptolemus is one of the worst. He is the son of Achilles. Thetis, Achilles' mother, knew it was prophesied that her son would die if he fought at Troy. She made him dress like a girl, call himself Pyrrha and hide with a load of other girls at the court of Lycomedes, king of Skyros. Achilles was eventually exposed by Odysseus, but not before the young warrior had impregnated Deidamea, the king's daughter. Because Achilles had called himself Pyrrha, this son was called Pyrrhus, which means 'flame-coloured' and probably refers to his fiery temperament rather than his hair colour (see How the Greeks Used Colour, page 44). When Pyrrhus arrives in Troy he is dubbed Neoptolemos, which means 'new warrior'.

Neoptolemus does not appear in the *Iliad* but does in other epics from the cycle. He is notorious for killing Hector's son, Astyanax, and slaughtering the boy's grandfather, old King Priam as he clings to the altar. From around 550 BCE, he suddenly appears on Greek vases beating Priam to death with the body of Astyanax. Earlier, in a memorable scene from the *Iliad*, Hector had told his wife Andromache that one day 'a bronze-clad Achaean will lead you weeping into captivity as his slave' (*Iliad* 6.454ff.). With horrible irony, that 'bronze-clad Achaean' is Neoptolemus, the murderer of her own dear son. Neoptolemus then goes on to sacrifice Priam's youngest daughter, Polyxena, to ensure a fair breeze home (just as Agamemnon sacrificed his own daughter Iphigenia at the start of the campaign).

Neoptolemus fathers eight children by a granddaughter of Heracles before hearing that Helen of Troy's daughter, Hermione, has married Orestes. Menelaus, the girl's father, had promised her to him, so Neoptolemus rushes to claim her. Orestes is having none of it and kills Neoptolemus while he clings to an altar, a fitting death for someone who has also killed suppliants. The playwrights Euripides and Sophocles tried to give his character more nuance, but for me I will always remember the lines from Virgil's *Aeneid* where Neoptolemus chases down one of Priam's young sons before bashing through a door with his axe. It conjures up Jack Nicholson maniacally crowing 'Here's Johnny!' in Stanley Kubrick's 1980 film *The Shining*.

 Neoptolemus slaughters Priam on a vase *c.*490 BCE, Naples

AENEAS

I'll come right out and say it: I love Aeneas. In fact, he is probably my favourite mythological hero. This is a very unusual opinion. Most people, especially women, hate him. 'How could he just abandon Dido like that?' they cry. 'He is such a —!' Here they pop in the noun of their choice and it is never complimentary. But Aeneas never promised Dido he would stay with her and their passion was engineered by a couple of goddesses (what's new?). When he was told to get on with his mission, he dutifully did so. 'But he's so boring!' my friends protest. It's true. The adjective most often used to describe him is *pius*, which can mean 'dutiful', 'devout', 'responsible', 'conscientious', all unexciting epithets. But let's face it: the world could do with more conscientious people and fewer who give in to their lusts and passions.

There are two main reasons I love Aeneas. The first and main one is Virgil. I am in awe of Homer. Ovid gives me shivers. But if stranded on a desert island with only one work from antiquity, it would be Virgil's *Aeneid*. It is beautiful in so many senses but especially the visual. If Virgil were alive today he would be a filmmaker like Stanley Kubrick, Peter Weir or Sergio Leone, some of my favourites. And I have only dipped my toe in the *Aeneid*. Some scholars spend their whole lives swimming in its ocean. The other reason I love Aeneas is a fresco from Pompeii that shows him stoically having an arrowhead removed. He is so brave and handsome.

I realize that the *Aeneid* was a work of propaganda for Octavian as he became the first Roman emperor, Augustus, but the account of Aeneas' escape from Troy in Book 2 is all I want from a narrative. The story starts with Juno, the Roman version of Hera, hounding Aeneas (although for once it's not because he is Zeus' illegitimate child). He flees burning Troy, carrying his lame father Anchises on his back and holding his son Ascanius by the hand. Unfortunately, he loses his wife, but that will be handy later when he must make an alliance with the Latin princess Lavinia in his homeland-to-be. Back in Troy, with the city still smoking, a few hundred refugees gather in a sacred grove on the slopes of Mount Ida. When they are sure the Greeks have gone, they cut down the nymph-trees to build ships. (The ships will be changed back into nymphs when they have completed their task.)

The first six books of the *Aeneid* echo the *Odyssey* as Aeneas and the remnant of Troy's inhabitants sail around looking for a new homeland. The second six books of the *Aeneid* imitate the *Iliad* as Aeneas battles Italian tribes who don't want him to make their territory his new Troy. Ursula K. Le Guin's 2008 novel *Lavinia* tells his story from a woman's point of view. Although the *Aeneid* ends abruptly, possibly because Virgil died before it was quite finished, we know the fate of Aeneas from other sources. He marries Lavinia, dies bravely in battle and becomes a local deity. More importantly, his son Ascanius founds a line of kings that will lead to Romulus, the founder and first king of Rome.

MIDAS

Midas isn't really a hero but he did give us the phrase 'Midas touch', meaning some-one who turns 'turns things to gold'. There was a real King Midas but Ovid's famous version of the story is about a mythical king (*Metamorphoses* 11.85ff.). It takes place in Phrygia, which is Anatolia, in what is now central Turkey. Midas was the legendary founder of Turkey's capital city Ankara. He was a wealthy king who showed kindness to Silenus, the foster father of Dionysus. In gratitude, Dionysus granted Midas one wish. Although he was already wealthy, Midas asked that everything he touched be turned to gold. Dionysus was peeved that the king had chosen such a selfish wish, but granted it anyway.

Turning things to gold was exciting for short time, until Midas grew hungry and realized he could neither eat nor drink. (The version where he accidentally turns his daughter to gold was an innovation of the American writer Nathaniel Hawthorne.) According to Aristotle, Midas starves to death (*Politics* 1257b). But in Ovid's version, Midas cries out to Dionysus to forgive him and reverse the curse. Dionysus sends word that he should bathe in the local river, the Pactolus, which from then on was famous for having gold dust in the sandy riverbed. Hugely relieved, Midas renounces his wealth and follows the god Pan, living among wild creatures in the woods.

Not long after, Pan challenges Apollo to a musical contest in which Pan will play his panpipes and Apollo his lyre. Everyone present, including the judge, the old mountain god Tmolus, declares Apollo's charming music to be better than Pan's rustic reeds. But Midas foolishly objects and calls the ruling unjust. Angry Apollo punishes Midas by turning his human ears into donkey ears, long and hairy. Humiliated, Midas returns home and hides his shameful new appendages beneath a turban. Only his barber knows the truth, and he has been sworn to secrecy. But the barber is desperate to tell someone, so he goes to a remote place, digs in the ground and whispers 'King Midas has ass's ears' into the hole. A year later, reeds have grown up from the hole and, when the wind rises in the reeds, they sound like panpipes. Travellers passing by seem to hear a song in the reeds: 'King Midas has ass's ears' (*Metamorphoses* 11.193ff.).

☞ Midas has ass's ears on a vase *c.*440 BCE, British Museum

HEROINES

Women had few rights in ancient Rome and Greece and were often dismissed as lesser creatures than men. Hesiod was a grumpy misogynist and seemed to blame women for everything. As previously mentioned, Zeus created Pandora and the race of women to be an evil for men (*Theogony* 700). But other more empathetic poets and tragedians like Homer, Sophocles, Euripides and Ovid, showed that women could also be respected and admired. Here are some examples.

ATALANTA

When Atalanta was born, her father exposed her because she was not a boy. This was a common fate of baby girls in ancient Greece and Rome. Instead of killing an unwanted child you would merely leave it somewhere in the wilderness. If it died, it was the gods' will and not your fault. In Atalanta's case, a she-bear found her and nursed her until some hunters took over parenting duties.

The girl grew up devoted to Artemis, goddess of the hunt, and became a skilled huntress and swift runner. She went with Jason on the *Argo* to capture the Golden Fleece, took part in the Calydonian Boar Hunt and wrestled Peleus (father of Achilles) and won. This last subject was popular on Greek vases. But she is probably best known for a footrace of love. Ovid tells that an oracle predicted disaster if she married. So she imposed a condition for suitors. They could only marry her if they beat her in a

footrace. And if they lost, they died. This successfully discouraged courtship until a young man named Hippomenes fell in love with the beautiful huntress. He begged Aphrodite for help, and she gave him three golden apples. Every time Atalanta overtook Hippomenes in the race, he would toss an apple behind him. Unable to resist a bright bauble, Atalanta took the bait – three times. Hippomenes won the race and her hand in marriage.

But Hippomenes, in his triumph, forgot to thank Aphrodite for her help, and the goddess made passion come upon them while they were hunting so that they made love in a sanctuary belonging to one of the gods. For this sacrilege they were turned into lions, which is how Ovid could include them in his *Metamorphoses*. It was not such a bad ending: now they could hunt together and mate whenever they liked.

ALCESTIS

Alcestis was the name of a beautiful princess of Thessaly, the daughter of King Pelias, the same king who sent Jason on a quest for the Golden Fleece. She married a man named Admetus, king of nearby Pherae, and they loved each other deeply. One day he fell sick. 'I am dying,' he told her. 'But Apollo likes me. He knew I was destined to die young, and he got the Fates drunk one day and made them promise that when my time had come, someone could take my place. I'll ask my old parents whether one of them will go to Hades instead of me.' But neither of Admetus' parents wanted to give their lives for his, nor did any of his friends. So Alcestis offered to die for him and 'to look no more on the light of the sun' (Euripides, *Alcestis* 1.18).

On the day she is to die, white-clad Apollo with his golden bow sees black-clad Thanatos (Death) approaching with his sword. After a short conversation, Apollo leaves, or else he will become polluted. Alcestis dies in the arms of Admetus, who is grief-stricken (though not enough to suffer the death meant for him). The house is in mourning when a visitor arrives. It is Heracles and he must be shown hospitality. When he finds out what has just occurred, he chases after Thanatos, wrestles him and brings Alcestis back to Admetus. For three days she cannot speak but then she recovers and the two of them live happily ever after.

Because this play has a happy ending, scholars wonder if the Athenians classed it as a tragedy. The story is a popular one and has been told in at least seven operas as well as in play form by the poet T.S. Eliot: *The Cocktail Party* premiered at the Edinburgh Festival in 1949.

ANTIGONE

Why is *Antigone* by Sophocles the most frequently performed Greek tragedy in the world today? Antigone was one of four children born of the incestuous union of Oedipus and his mother Jocasta. In Sophocles' play, both her parents are now dead and her brothers are warring with each other about which of them should rule Thebes. The brothers kill each other in their struggle for the crown and it goes instead to their uncle Creon. He buries the one who fought on the side of Thebes but forbids anyone to bury the other brother. One of the worst things you could do in the ancient world was to leave a loved one unburied. The body would be food for dogs, birds and worms, and the soul would wander the banks of the river Styx with no way of getting across, dishonoured for all eternity. The young Antigone defies the powerful King Creon's wishes and buries her brother. She is caught by a soldier and her punishment is dreadful. Her own uncle seals her in an underground tomb so that she will starve to death. Later he repents, only to find she has hung herself. Although the play ends tragically, Antigone's brave stand against tyranny has made a change and brought some justice to her world.

French playwright Jean Anouilh's retelling of the story was staged in 1944, in Nazi-occupied Paris, and Nelson Mandela played Creon in a version of Sophocles' play put on in the 1960s during his time in prison. An acclaimed modern retelling is the novel *Home Fire* (2017) by Kamila Shamsie. I asked my friends – many of whom are Classics teachers or writers – why they thought Sophocles' *Antigone* was so popular and I got many excellent answers: 'It's one of the most school-friendly'; 'It was unusual to have a female protagonist back then, and in fact it still is unusual today'; 'Hegel used it to illustrate his theory of history'; 'It captures the key themes I need to teach of *nomos* vs *physis* and *polis* vs *oikos*'; 'Intergenerational conflict is always relevant'; 'Conflict of loyalty to family vs loyalty to state continues to resonate'; 'The ideas are readily transferable to modern circumstances'. I noticed that most of their answers mentioned conflict, relevance and an appealing protagonist. But the best answer was the simplest: 'A teenage girl speaks truth to power.'

PENTHESILEA

Penthesilea was queen of the Amazons, a race of women warriors, during the Trojan War. Her story was first told in a lost epic poem called the *Aethiopis*, part of the Epic Cycle (see page 161). In that version she is from Thrace, a country which usually stood for strangeness and barbarity in Greek thought. The story goes that she and a dozen of her fellow Amazons came to help the Trojans. They bravely battle the Greeks, but finally Penthesilea faces the great Achilles and he kills her.

In some versions of the myth, the opponents' eyes lock at the moment of her death and they fall in love. In other tellings, it is only after Achilles removes her helmet and sees her face, or even strips her of her armour and gazes upon her naked body, that he falls in love. In one version, the ugly Greek Thersites taunts Achilles for loving a dead Amazon and, in anger, Achilles slaughters him. A modern poem called 'Penthesilea' by the *I, Claudius* author, Robert Graves, possibly throws light on a darker subtext with a mention of necrophilia.

Alternate versions of her story bring Penthesilea from Anatolia, and some make Neoptolemus, the son of Achilles, her killer. Later, the Latin poet Virgil introduces his own version of Penthesilea, a Latin princess named Camilla. She fights the Trojans and dies, but never comes face to face with Aeneas, who is destined to marry Lavinia. One of the great masterpieces of Greek art is a black-figure amphora by Exekias, now in the British Museum. It shows Achilles at the moment he stabs a swooning Penthesilea. His Corinthian-style helmet shows only his eyes, which are locked with hers. Her face is uncovered and her mouth is slightly open as she gazes back up at him. This used to be my favourite Greek vase, until Robert Graves ruined it for me.

☞ Achilles kills Penthesilea on the Exekias Amphora *c.*535 BCE, British Museum

PENELOPE

Odysseus was the cleverest of the Greeks. Before the Trojan War he went to Sparta to vie with other Greeks to win the hand of Helen, but spotted lovely Penelope, another Spartan princess, and cleverly contrived to obtain her as his wife instead (see page 178).

Penelope became an archetype of the faithful and long-suffering wife. She bears Odysseus one son, Telemachus, before he goes off to the Trojan War. In the last few years of his 20-year absence, she is pestered by over a hundred suitors who want to marry her and claim the kingdom of Ithaca for themselves. Penelope, whose name might mean 'face of a weaver', tells the suitors she will make her choice when she has finished weaving a shroud for her father-in-law. But Penelope's cunning rivals that of her husband Odysseus, and although she weaves conspicuously by day, each night she secretly unpicks what she has woven. Betrayed by one of her servant girls, she sets a final competition: she will marry whichever of the suitors can string the bow of Odysseus and shoot an arrow through 12 axes.

That very night an old beggar appears, claiming to be her long-lost husband. Even after Athena has removed the beggar's disguise and made him look godlike, Penelope is not sure if it is really Odysseus. She tells a servant girl to move their bed, but Odysseus made the bed himself and knows that one post is made from a live olive tree, so it cannot be moved. When he tells her this, she is finally convinced. Odysseus strings the bow (which only he can do), kills all the suitors and they live happily ever after...or at least for a few more years until he goes wandering again.

Penelope as faithfully waiting wife was a popular subject on Greek vases and signet rings. She is often shown head covered and resting her cheek on her hand, with her bent elbow propped on her crossed legs (to show that nobody is getting in there!). Sometimes there is a basket of wool beneath her chair, and sometimes her loom looms behind her.

HELEN OF TROY

I'm going to call her Helen of Troy even though she was born, bred and married in Sparta. Helen had an astonishing conception and an extraordinary life. Remember when Zeus became a swan and seduced or raped Leda (see page 15)? One of his off-spring by her was a girl named Helen. By the age of ten, her beauty was already so famous that Theseus decided to abduct her and make her his wife. He stashed her with his mother Aethra while he went off on another quest. Helen's brothers, Castor and Polydeuces (page 149), rescued her and made Aethra her slave.

Back in Sparta, some fifty kings came to vie for Helen's hand in marriage. They all brought gifts to her reputed father, Tyndareus, the city's king – all except Odysseus, who astutely reasoned he had no chance of winning her hand, and who instead had his eyes on Penelope, Tyndareus' niece. 'Help me win Penelope,' he said to Tyndareus, 'and I will share my idea of how you can prevent any future squabbles over your daughter.' His plan was to make all the suitors swear a solemn oath that, if anyone should try to abduct Helen, they would all band together to rescue her. All the suitors duly swore the oath, and the winner was then announced as Menelaus, the exiled son of Atreus. Helen, probably only 13 or 14 at this time, had no say in the matter.

Helen bore Menelaus a daughter, Hermione, but then came a handsome young stranger from the east. His name was Paris, and Aphrodite had promised him Helen as his reward for choosing her as the most beautiful (see page 39). In some accounts, Helen finally gets some agency and goes willingly, but in other versions she is once again taken against her will. In what may be the oldest depiction of this, on a Geometric vase in the British Museum, a man is shown grasping a woman by the wrist and leading her into a many-oared galley.

As portrayed by Homer, Helen is not merely beautiful but also extremely percep-tive. She realizes the consequences of her departure with Paris and regrets them, often chiding Paris for his cheerfully oblivious nature. She plays both sides, sometimes col-laborating with Greeks such as Odysseus when he sneaks into Troy, but also charming Priam, even though she will be the death of him and all his sons. She gives a beautiful description of Odysseus when pointing out the Greeks to Priam from the walls of Troy.

☞ Helen, Eros and Menelaus on a vase c.445 BCE, Louvre

She tells Priam that Odysseus stands stiffly when making speeches so that one might think him a fool. 'But when he lets his great voice loose from his chest his words fall like stormy snowflakes, and no other mortal can compete with him' (*Iliad* 3.222). In a memorable scene from the *Odyssey*, Menelaus recalls how Helen walked around the Trojan Horse three times, imitating the voices of all the different wives of the Greeks, trying to tempt them to give themselves away (*Odyssey* 4.265ff.).

When, after ten years of battle, suffering and death, Troy is finally taken, Menelaus stalks through the burning city, searching for Helen. But as he approaches her with drawn sword and murder in his eyes, she pulls aside her garments to show him her breasts. Menelaus is so overcome by her beauty that he lets his sword fall and embraces her. The two of them eventually return to Sparta and live happily ever after. In one way, it seems utterly unfair, but in another I am proud of Helen. You go, girl!

There is also a variation of the myth where Paris only got a simulacrum of Helen and the real Helen of Sparta waited out the war in Egypt. But I hold no truck with these simulacra!

PROCNE

For balance, here is Procne, who may properly be termed an anti-heroine: another parent who served up her child as a meal, in an even more horrible story than that of Tantalus and Pelops. The Athenian princess Procne marries Tereus (who is the real bad guy in this horror story). Tereus takes his bride Procne back to his homeland of Thrace, and in due time she gives birth to a beautiful little boy. After about five years, Procne misses her sister Philomela and begs Tereus to bring her to visit. Tereus rapes Philomela, cuts out her tongue, locks her up and continues to abuse her. Unable to speak, Philomela weaves a tapestry telling what has happened to her. 'She wove purple symbols [*purpureas notas*] into a white cloth,' says Ovid (*Metamorphoses* 6.577). Sophocles, in his lost tragedy *Tereus*, calls the tapestry 'the voice of the shuttle' (Aristotle, *Poetics* 1454b 14ff.).

Philomela gives the rolled-up tapestry to a servant girl who brings it to Procne. When Procne unrolls it, she is stunned with grief and rage. She dresses as a follower of Dionysus, rescues her sister and brings her home, also in disguise. Trying to find the worst revenge possible, Procne kills her little son by Tereus. Then she and Philomela serve him up to Tereus at a special banquet. Tereus eats with gusto and when he asks where his little boy is, Procne says 'Inside you!' and Philomela thrusts the child's bloody head into his face. With a roar of rage and anguish, Tereus draws his sword and charges at them.

At that moment, all three are changed into birds. Tereus into the hoopoe with its crest like a warrior's helmet and its beak like a sword, Philomela into a voiceless swallow and Procne into a nightingale. Ovid has it the other way round, making Procne the swallow wheeling round and round the palace, and Philomela, with tongue restored, the nightingale. Either way, the ancient Greeks and Romans obviously didn't know that it is only the male nightingale, not the female, that sings. For the full video-nasty horror of this story, read the chilling translation of Ovid's version by Ted Hughes in his *Tales of Ovid* (1997).

MONSTERS
& HYBRIDS

The world of ancient Graeco-Roman mythology is full of monsters and hybrids, which were either born that way or transformed, often as punishment for outrageous behaviour. There are also several proto-robots, mostly created by Hephaestus.

Scylla on a vase *c.*470 BCE, Louvre

THREE TYPES OF CYCLOPES

The Greek word *kyklopes* means 'circle-eyes' and there are three different versions of these monsters in Greek mythology. The first ones we meet are three sons of Gaia and Uranus. They later forge Zeus' thunderbolts and their names reflect this: Arges (Bright), Brontes (Thunder) and Steropes (Lightning). These three Cyclopes help Zeus, unlike the ones in Homer's *Odyssey* who clash with Odysseus on his way home from Troy. Those ones are lawless shepherds who live in caves and are children of Poseidon. In one of the best-known tales from the *Odyssey*, a Cyclops named Polyphemus refuses hospitality to Odysseus and his men, and instead traps them in his cave and begins to devour them, until Odysseus devises a clever plan to escape. The final class of Cyclopes are builders big enough to have carried massive stones to build the walls of Mycenae, Tiryns and Argos. One mythographer tells us that Perseus brought them home with him to help build up those very towns.

SCYLLA & CHARYBDIS

The expression 'between Scylla and Charybdis' is still used to describe a choice between two bad outcomes. Scylla and Charybdis were two sea monsters in close geographical proximity to each other. Imagine Italy as a high-heeled, thigh-high boot kicking the football of Sicily. Scylla lived on the toe of Italy and Charybdis in the water near the facing coast of Sicily, only a few miles away. Odysseus had to sail this stretch of sea, now known as the Straits of Messina. He chose to go closer to Scylla, a fish-woman with several ravenous dogs' heads, who grabbed half a dozen of his men as they passed by. That was a bad enough outcome, but better than losing his whole ship to the whirlpool Charybdis. Some accounts have Scylla born as a monster, but later writers accuse Circe of changing a beautiful nymph into the horrid creature because she was jealous. Charybdis also started life as a woman and in one version she was turned into a whirlpool by Zeus as punishment for stealing some cattle.

MEDUSA & THE GORGONS

Hesiod tells us that three sisters called the Gorgons lived at the edge of the world near the night. Two, Stheno and Euryale, were immortal but Medusa was not. She lay with the 'Blue-Haired One' (Poseidon) in a soft flower-studded meadow, and some time later, when Perseus cut off her head, two creatures sprang forth: Chrysaor, a giant with a golden sickle, and Pegasus, a winged horse (*Theogony* 280ff.). Later poets say she was a beautiful woman who slept with Poseidon not in a flowery meadow but in Athena's temple. This enraged the goddess of wisdom and she punished Medusa by making her hideously ugly with snake hair and a gaze that could literally petrify you. She was later famously slain by Perseus and her fiercesome head incorporated into Athena's aegis (see page 32).

Scary faces staring out at the viewer were apotropaic, a primitive way of keeping away evil spirits or reflecting back the evil eye. My unproven instinct is that the myth of Medusa arose to explain these frightening faces with their malevolent gaze. She was memorably portrayed in the 1981 movie *Clash of the Titans*, the last film to feature the stop-motion animation of Ray Harryhausen. In the 2022 novel *Stone Blind*, Natalie Haynes makes Medusa a sympathetic victim of assault by Poseidon.

THE EVIL EYE

As in many ancient cultures, the ancient Greeks and Romans believed in the evil eye. This arose from the primitive fear of being spotted by a predator, but also from their idea of how vision worked. Extramission was the idea that the eye sent out little particles to see the things around it. Intromission was the idea that objects were constantly shedding their atom-thick layer of outer essence and sending it into the eyes of those around. Either way, there are 'beams' in or out of the eye. Because of this, it was believed that someone could look at you with evil intent and bring on sickness or even death. Charms and amulets with another eye or face looking back could 'deflect' this evil beam. We see this clearly in an account of Medea defeating Talos (see page 190). Apollonius of Rhodes even adds this: 'Father Zeus, a terrible thought has come to mind: not only by sickness and wounds does destruction meet us, but that someone can harm us from a distance' (*Argonautica* 4.1673ff.).

HARPIES & SIRENS

There are two classes of creatures who are half-woman, half-bird. Harpies were originally personifications of blustery north winds but they morphed into hybrid women-birds. Their name comes from the Greek verb *harpazo*, meaning 'to snatch'. They are sent by the gods to torment impious mortals. Their most famous victim is the prophet Phineas from the story of Jason and the Argonauts. A red-figure vase in the Getty Villa, Malibu, painted *c.*480 BCE, shows the Harpies as women with wings. They swoop down to steal the food laid before blind, old Phineas who holds up his arms to ward them off. One of their most memorable appearances in modern times is in Philip Pullman's *His Dark Materials*, where the Harpies feature as the terrifying guardians of the Land of the Dead.

Sirens form the other class of bird-women. They sit on craggy islands and sing irresistible songs, thus luring sailors to their death on the rocks. The Sirens are first outwitted by Jason and his Argonauts, who get their onboard musician Orpheus to play music that will drown out their song. But their most famous encounter is with Odysseus on his way home from Troy. He has been forewarned and makes his men plug their ears with wax and then bind him to the ship's mast with orders not to untie him until they are well past the deadly island. This means that he alone hears their 'Siren Song' and survives. We can see what one Corinthian potter thought these creatures looked like on a vase of *c.*550 BCE in the Louvre. They have the bodies of birds and heads of women. In later times, Sirens are often portrayed as sexy mermaids.

🐦 Siren on a vase *c.*550 BCE, Louvre

TALOS

I was nine years old when I first saw the 1963 film *Jason and the Argonauts*. Many scenes will stay with me but none as vividly as when the gigantic bronze statue of a crouching man slowly turns his head to stare at the Argonauts with terrifying empty eyes. Then he gets down off his plinth and stomps after them, only stopped when Jason pulls a plug from his heel and lets out his steaming *ichor* (divine blood). Weakened by this loss of vital juices, he sways and then crashes to the ground.

According to the ancient authors, Talos was either a last remnant of a man from the Age of Bronze or a creation of Hephaestus, made to protect Europa on her island home of Crete. Being a giant, he was able to patrol the island's perimeter three times a day. In the *Argonautica*, an epic poem by Apollonius of Rhodes written in the 3rd century BCE, when Talos saw the *Argo* approaching, he threw great rocks at it. In this telling, it is not one of the Argonauts who defeats him, but rather Medea. She curses Talos and then gives him the evil eye. 'Concentrating on evil, she bewitched the eyeballs of bronze Talos with her hostile gaze' (*Argonautica* 4.1669ff.). In this version, he staggers and falls and scratches his vulnerable heel on a sharp rock, allowing the *ichor* to flow out.

Talos is not always a giant – the word 'giant' simply means offspring of Gaia. On one vase, a human-sized Talos sinks backwards with liquid coming from his eye, possibly to show he is wounded by Medea's gaze. Silver coins of the 3rd century BCE from Crete show Talos ready to throw a rock at enemy ships and sporting wings, possibly to indicate his speedy circuits of the island.

Winged Talos with rock on a Cretan coin *c.*290 BCE, Louvre

THE MINOTAUR

The Minotaur is literally the bull (*tauros*) of Minos. You don't want to know how this creature came into existence...Let us just say a baby with a bull's head must have hurt his mother Pasiphaë when he was born. She named him Asterion. Ovid wrote this line about the minotaur, '*Semibovemque virum semivirumque bovem*', a Latin tongue-twister that means 'a half-bull man and a half-man bull' – a hybrid line for a hybrid creature (*Ars Amatoria* 2.24).

An object of shame to his mother's husband, Minos, king of Crete, he was shut away in an underground maze (the labyrinth) and fed on human sacrifices. His half-sister Ariadne betrayed him with a ball of twine, and when he met Theseus he met his doom (see page 150). He is sometimes portrayed as an almost sympathetic character, a misfit who has been abandoned and abused, and on one vase his mother cradles toddler Asterion on her lap.

LABYRINTH & LABRYS

The Greek word for maze is *labyrinthos* and the story of Theseus entering a maze to kill the Minotaur goes back to at least the 3rd century BCE. According to the myth, the labyrinth was built by Daedalus as a place where the Cretan King Minos could hide his wife's shameful offspring. In Roman times, people searched for the labyrinth without luck although coins with a maze on one side kept turning up at a place called Knossos. It was not until 1878 that a Greek businessman named Minos Kalokairinos dug at Knossos and uncovered foundations of a vast Bronze Age building with maze-like foundations, frescoes of bull leapers and graffiti scratched on the walls. Not long after, British archaeologist Arthur Evans managed to buy part of the land for his own excavations. Noticing that some of the images scratched on the walls were of double axes, he remembered a single occurrence of the word *labrys* in Plutarch, who claimed it was Lydian for 'double axe' (*Quaestiones Graecae* 45). Evans controversially declared that the word 'labyrinth' meant 'House of the Double Axes' and that this was the long-lost Palace of Minos.

CERBERUS

Better known today as 'Fluffy', the hellhound from the book and film of *Harry Potter and the Philosopher's Stone* (1997 and 2001), Cerberus is the watchdog of the underworld, but with a wicked twist. He'll happily let you in, but letting you out is another matter. The first time we meet Cerberus, in Hesiod's *Theogony*, he has a taste for raw flesh, a brazen bark and a mind-boggling 50 heads. Pindar ups the ante by giving him 100 heads. But after that, most ancient storytellers and artists settle for giving him just three. Sometimes snakes are added, so he has a bizarre combination of dog and snake heads. A charming red-figure vase shows Heracles crouching down and letting an almost cuddly Cerberus – with only two heads and a couple of snakes – sniff his fingers (apparently the best way to approach a strange dog). A marvellous Etruscan vase (see page 145) shows Cerberus with three different-coloured heads; this gave me the idea for the canine murder victims in my first book, *The Thieves of Ostia* (2001).

AFTERWORD

Humans are sentient beings, driven by animal instincts we can barely control, painfully aware of our mortality, telling stories to distract and comfort ourselves. The most basic stories are the myths. The gods are personified natural forces as well as personified abstract concepts. The gods also let us examine cultural archetypes: the stern father, the self-sacrificing mother, the patient or vengeful wife, the preferred older sibling, the neglected younger one, the misfit, the jealous one, the unmarried aunt, the charming uncle, the angry cousin, the outcast, the bully, the joker, the daydreamer, the artist.

Myths help us explore our taboos and passions, our desire for sex, our craving for justice, our terror of the indifferent predator that devours us alive. Myths explain the wonders of the world: springs of water that rise from between rocks; the sky with its clouds, lightning, thunder, wind and rainbows; the sea with its depths, waves, tsunamis and changes of colour; the surreal variety of animals from spider mites to chameleons to bulls. Myths in the form of tragic dramas bring catharsis: a cleansing surge of pity, horror and even laughter that helps bring our emotions back into balance. Myths offer consolation that others have known greater losses, made more terrible mistakes, suffered more crushing indignities, experienced deeper agonies. Myths re-enacted in mystery cults bring us closer to the gods and show the soul the way to go after death. They promise a possible reward for our suffering: a home in the stars or some idyllic garden in the afterlife.

Humans have been called *Homo narrans* ('storytelling man') or even *Pan narrans* ('storytelling ape'). Myths will always be told and retold, until that long-predicted day comes when 'the sea and the land and the dome of the sky will catch fire and burn, and the heavy mass of the world will suffer' (Ovid, *Metamorphoses* 1.256ff.).

Fresco of Apollo with lyre, 1st century CE, Palatine Museum, Rome

SOURCES

Here are some of the main sources that supply us with information about the gods and goddesses, starting with the oldest.

HOMER'S ILIAD (C.700 BCE)

'Rage! Sing about the rage of Achilles, Goddess: the destructive rage of the son of Peleus...' This hugely influential ancient epic poem covers just over a month in the ten-year war between the Greeks and Trojans. It recounts the anger of the Greek warrior Achilles at his fellow Greek leaders and at his Trojan enemies, especially the warrior Hector, who has killed his best friend. It is considered by some to be the first great masterpiece of Western fiction. Although we call it Homer's *Iliad*, nobody knows who Homer was, or even if there was just one poet. All we know is that in pre-literate times this poem was memorized and recited and that, soon after the Greeks got an alphabet, it was written down.

HOMER'S ODYSSEY (C.700 BCE)

'Tell me, Muse, about that crafty man who was driven far and wide after he destroyed Troy...' What happened to the Greek hero Odysseus after the end of the Trojan War? The *Odyssey* starts with his son Telemachus asking this question, then jumps to Odysseus recounting the good stuff: his ten-year voyage home encountering man-eating monsters and beautiful sorceresses. It finishes with Odysseus' famous homecoming and his slaughter of the men and women who have been taking advantage of his faithful wife Penelope.

HESIOD'S THEOGONY (C.700 BCE)

'Let us begin to sing, inspired by the Muses of Mount Helicon...' Less exciting and less read than Homer, Hesiod lived around the same time (maybe even earlier) and also wrote epic poems. The *Theogony* (not necessarily his choice of title) is his tale of how the gods came to be, and as our earliest literary account of the mythical cosmogony, it is hugely important. It is from him that we get the succession myth of Uranus to Cronus to Zeus and all the gods, Titans and monsters produced as a result.

FAMOUS VASE PAINTERS

Ancient vases are one of our most plentiful sources of information about the gods and goddesses. Although mainly Athenian, we also get examples from Corinth and Magna Graecia (the Greek-speaking parts of Italy). The artists who decorated them sometimes show myths that have not survived in other sources, expand those that have, or provide different versions. A few vase painters signed their work and so we know their names, but experts can identify anonymous craftsmen by their style and often name them after an outstanding piece. Here are a few masters of the craft mentioned in this book, listed chronologically:

Sophilos – active in Athens in the early 6th century BCE, he is the earliest painter known by name. He worked in black-figure with added touches of colour, and was not just a painter but a potter. The so-called Sophilos Dinos, a wine-mixing bowl in the British Museum, is one of my favourite sources.

Exekias – active in Athens in the mid-6th century BCE, he worked mainly in black-figure and, like Sophilos, was a potter as well as painter. He was the Shakespeare of vase painters. He painted two of my favourite vase – the Exekias Amphora in the British Museum, which shows Achilles falling in love with Penthesilea at the very moment he kills her, and a *kylix* (drinking cup) in the Museum Antiker Kleinkunst, Munich, showing Dionysus and the pirates-turned-dolphins.

The Berlin Painter – active in Athens in the early 5th century BC, he worked in red-figure. We do not know his name, so his nickname derives from a lidded amphora in the Altes Museum, Berlin, depicting Hermes and satyrs.

HESIOD'S WORKS AND DAYS (C. 700 BCE)

'Muses of Mount Pieria, glorious in song, come tell of your father Zeus...' *Works and Days* is a 'didactic poem' which means it teaches you something using a poetic format. Essentially, it is a peevish rebuke addressed to Hesiod's layabout brother Perses, tacked on to a 'farmers' almanac' in epic verse. So we get lines like 'Perses, take my advice to heart: don't let mischievous Strife hold you back from work by tempting you to listen to the wrangles of the courthouse', as well as 'Pray to Zeus of the Earth and to pure Demeter...when first you begin ploughing'. However, the poem also contains some interesting stories from the Greek cosmogony: the tale of Prometheus, Epimetheus and Pandora, and the Ages of Man.

AESOP'S FABLES (C.600 BCE ONWARDS)

If Homer and Hesiod are high-brow, Aesop is most definitely low-brow. A deformed enslaved person born in the hinterland of the Greek world, he composed short fables in prose, the opposite of long poetic epics. Although he comes between Homer and Plato, living between 620 and 560 BCE, the earliest written versions don't appear until three centuries later, and then keep arriving in both Greek and Latin well into the medieval period. As Mark Twain is to quotations, Aesop is to fables. His name attracts them, as a magnet attracts iron filings. Although his best-known fables deal with ordinary people and extraordinary animals, the gods appear frequently, too.

LYRIC POETRY (7TH–5TH CENTURY BCE)

Pindar and Bacchylides were two of the most famous of the Nine Lyric Poets. Lyric poetry was essentially songs sung to the lyre, and much shorter than epic poetry. Sappho, the famous female poet, was one of the Nine, but only a few poems and fragments of hers have survived.

HERODOTUS' HISTORIES (5TH CENTURY BCE)

Fondly called the Father of History, Herodotus was the first to write history rather than poetry. He often includes facts about the gods, who were an embedded part of daily life in ancient Greece.

ATHENIAN DRAMA (500–300 BCE)

Say it with me: ACE! (spelled ASE) – Aeschylus, Sophocles, Euripides. They are the three great tragedians, writing (musical and masked) plays to compete in a festival to Dionysus. These playwrights mostly retold stories from Greek mythology. At least a dozen new plays were written every year, although fewer than 50 have survived. For example, we know Sophocles wrote between 120 and 130 plays, but only 7 have come down to us intact. As a postscript there is the wonderful Aristophanes, who wrote satiric comedies. His plays show the gentler side of the gods and goddesses. In his comedy *The Frogs* (performed 405 BCE), he has an amusing Dionysus travel to the underworld to bring back Athens' greatest tragedian in order to encourage the citizens.

PLATO'S DIALOGUES (C 4TH CENTURY BCE)

The philosopher Plato has lots to say about myths. He even invented some, including the Myth of Atlantis and the Myth of Er. Plato strongly disapproved of Homer and Hesiod, claiming that they sometimes showed the gods behaving badly, which risked corrupting the youth. In Plato's *Republic* (*c.*375 BCE), for example, Socrates, who had been Plato's teacher and is the main character in most of his dialogues, criticizes Homer's Zeus for lusting after Hera so passionately that he forgets everything else (*Iliad* 14.294ff.). And Socrates claims that Achilles was greedy in accepting gifts from Agamemnon and a ransom for Hector's body (*Republic* 3.390e). Plato's idea of punishment and reward in the afterlife is startling in its anticipation of a Christian concept of Heaven and Hell (*Republic*).

ARISTOTLE'S POLITICS AND POETICS (4TH CENTURY BCE)

One of the greatest thinkers of all time, the Greek philosopher Aristotle studied under Plato and taught Alexander the Great. He set up his own school in Athens and wrote prodigiously about many topics including biology, metaphysics and how to live a good life. One of his most famous treatises is the *Politics*, on how people can best live in society. Another is an analysis of drama, the *Poetics*, written around 330 BCE and still read by many Hollywood screenwriters today.

APOLLONIUS OF RHODES' ARGONAUTICA (3ʳᴰ CENTURY BCE)

Apollonius' account of Jason and the Argonauts is full of information about the gods and many heroes.

VIRGIL'S AENEID (1ˢᵀ CENTURY BCE)

Publius Vergilius Maro, better known as Virgil, was perhaps the greatest poet of ancient Rome, best known for the *Aeneid*, an epic poem in dactylic hexameter, commissioned by Octavian (soon to be known as Augustus). Although the epic was intended to help Octavian secure power after a lengthy and bloody civil war, Virgil put great care into it, polishing each line over and over like a mother bear licking her cubs. Virgil was deeply influenced by Homer but never plagiarized him, quipping that 'it would be easier to steal the club of Hercules than a single line of Homer' (*Vita Suetonii-Donati* 22–4). The *Aeneid* was not quite finished when, in 19 BCE, Virgil fell ill with a fever. His dying request was that it be burned. Thankfully, his wishes were ignored, and the epic poem has become an acknowledged masterpiece of Western literature, inspiring Dante and many others.

OVID'S METAMORPHOSES (1ˢᵀ CENTURY BCE)

Publius Ovidius Naso, aka Ovid, was a brilliant Roman poet who has been crucial in the modern reception of Graeco-Roman mythology (see page 21). His masterpiece, *The Metamorphoses* , or 'The Changes', is a long poetic account of the origin of the cosmos and the gods and goddesses who followed, all united by the theme of change. Hugely popular in his time and for many (but not all) periods after, this is one of the top sources of Greek myths and an acknowledged masterpiece. The English poet Ted Hughes translated a selection of the poems in his book *Tales from Ovid* (1997). If you are interested, start there. We can also learn a great deal about the Greek myths from Ovid's other works, such as the epistolary *Heroides* and the *Fasti*, a poem detailing the origins of Roman holidays and customs.

PLUTARCH'S PARALLEL LIVES (1ST CENTURY CE)

A Greek historian and philosopher living in the Roman period, Plutarch came up with the clever idea of matching notable Romans with their earlier Greek counterparts. He mostly pairs real historical figures such as Alexander the Great and Julius Caesar, but his first duo is a mythical one: Theseus, the founder of Athens, goes with Romulus, the founder of Rome. Plutarch's story about Pan being dead (see page 127) comes from a collection of essays called *Moralia*.

APOLLODORUS' BIBLIOTHECA (1ST–2ND CENTURY CE)

Apollodorus, aka Pseudo-Apollodorus, was a Greek living in the Roman period who wrote in Greek, the lingua franca of the time. He wrote a guide to Greek mythology called the *Bibliotheca*, or 'Library', summarizing all the myths from creation onwards. Sadly, his account ends with Theseus, where our surviving manuscripts peter out.

APULEIUS' METAMORPHOSES (2ND CENTURY CE)

Born in the Roman province of Numidia (modern Algeria), Apuleius lived from *c.*124 to 170 CE. He travelled widely, was initiated into several mystery cults and wrote in Latin. He is most famous for his novel *Metamorphoses* (or *The Golden Ass*), in which a rich young man is transformed into a donkey by a spell gone wrong and has many adventures before he is restored to his human shape. Various tales are told during the course of the novel. One of them is that of Cupid and Psyche.

PAUSANIAS' DESCRIPTION OF GREECE (2ND CENTURY CE)

A geographer who wrote the first surviving travel guide, Pausanias is often our only source for which sanctuaries were devoted to which gods.

INDEX

AUTHOR'S ACKNOWLEDGEMENTS

I would like to thank commissioning editor Ellie Corbett (who has a soft spot for Hades) for inviting me to write this book. Also Flora Kirk (a fan of Mercury) for agreeing to illustrate it. Deep gratitude to my classics-loving colleagues and friends, many of whom I grilled about their favourite divinities. Special thanks to Professor Katherine Harloe, Director of the Institute of Classical Studies (fave goddess Thetis), along with her two daughters Alice (team Athena) and Izzy (team Artemis); they looked over an early proof. Praise to Professor Paul Cartledge, (prefers Odysseus' dog Argus to any of the gods), who also made many helpful comments and corrections. Shout-out to everyone at the Institute of Classical Studies Library, especially Sue Willetts (favours Athena) and Paul Jackson (likes Hermes). Katrina Kelly, founder of the Lytham St Annes Classical Association (another fan of Artemis), helped lots, as did poetess and lecturer Emily Lord-Kambitsch (Hecate fan), who proposed the idea of Hades as an administrator. I love you all.

ABOUT THE AUTHOR

Caroline Lawrence is the best-selling author of over 40 children's books, including her 17-book Roman Mysteries series. Born in London and raised in California, she spent hours leafing through her mother's art books, full of images from Greek mythology. After reading *The Last of the Wine* by Mary Renault and Homer's *Iliad* on her gap year, she studied Classics at Berkeley, then won a Marshall Scholarship to Cambridge. There, at Newnham College, she studied Classical Art and Archaeology. After Cambridge, Caroline remained in England and later took an MA in Hebrew and Jewish Studies at University College, London. She taught Latin and art at a London primary school for ten years before her light-bulb moment of writing 'Nancy Drew in ancient Rome' became a series of books for kids set in the ancient world. The Roman Mysteries books were televised by the BBC in 2007 and 2008. In 2009, Caroline won the Classical Association Prize for 'a significant contribution to the public understanding of Classics'. Since then, she has written more books set in the ancient world including The Roman Quests, a four-book sequel to The Roman Mysteries set in Roman Britain. She has also written two time-travel books and two retellings of stories from Virgil's *Aeneid*. Her illustrated books for middle-grade readers include a retelling of Aesop's Fables and a book about tropes from myths and movies called *How to Write a Great Story*. Caroline is passionate about story structure and often goes into schools to speak about myths, movies and storytelling.

ABOUT THE ILLUSTRATOR

Flora Kirk is a UK-based illustrator specializing in visual depictions of ancient Mediterranean civilizations. She loves to create art inspired by archaeology sites, ancient myths and visuals that echo the people of the past. After receiving her BA in Ancient Studies from the University of Maryland, Baltimore County, Flora spent a year in Cluj-Napoca, Romania, researching Roman coin imagery with the Fulbright Program. The following year, she completed an MA in Museum Studies at the University of Durham. She now lives in Newcastle upon Tyne, close to Hadrian's Wall, from where she focuses on bringing local museum archaeology collections back to life through illustration. Her recent projects include *The Roman Baths: Activity Book* with the Roman Baths Museum, and the Roman Border Gallery at Tullie House Museum and Art Gallery.